10

MINUTE GUIDE TO

SMART
BORROWING

by Barbara Hetzer

W9-CXQ-921

Macmillan Spectrum/Alpha

A Division of Macmillan Publishing
A Simon & Schuster Macmillan Company
1633 Broadway, New York, NY 10019-6785

International Standard Book Number: 0-02-861178-0
Library of Congress Catalog Card Number: 96-068539

98 97 96 10 9 8 7 6 5 4 3 2 1

Interpretation of the printing code: the rightmost double-digit number is the year of the book's first printing; the rightmost single-digit number is the number of the book's printing. For example, a printing code of 96-1 shows that this copy of the book was printed during the first printing of the book in 1996.

Printed in the United States of America

Publisher: Theresa Murtha
Development Editor: Debra Wishik Englander
Production Editor: Carol Sheehan
Cover Designer: Dan Armstrong
Designer: Barbara Kordesh
Indexer: Kevin Fulcher
Production Team: Heather Butler, Angela Calvert, Tricia Flodder, Beth Rago, Christy Wagner

CONTENTS

INTRODUCTION

Maybe you're in the market for a red convertible. Or that dream house with the white picket fence. Maybe you're even thinking about starting your own catering business. Or maybe you want to buy some hot new technology stocks. Where will you get the money to fund such purchases? No doubt, you'll borrow it.

In years past, you would've marched down to your friendly neighborhood bank and asked for a loan. You can still do that today, of course, but it may no longer be the best deal in town. There are many other sources, in fact, that you can tap to secure those funds. Did you know, for instance, that you can borrow money—often at very competitive rates—from your life insurance policy, your credit union, and even your retirement plan?

Which is the smarter choice? That depends upon what you want to buy, how much you want to borrow, and when you plan on paying it back. Are you borrowing to invest in a tangible asset, such as a house, that your family will live in for years to come? Or are you borrowing to finance a Paris vacation that'll soon leave you with nothing to show for it but a handful of pictures and some fond memories?

In this book, you'll learn everything you need to know about borrowing money, such as when it's smarter to choose an adjustable interest rate rather than a fixed rate. You'll learn why a 40-year mortgage is almost never a good deal and a three-year car loan almost always is. You'll learn the difference between borrowing to invest and borrowing to spend; a mortgage broker and a mortgage banker; and a home equity loan and a home equity line of credit.

You'll learn about points, margin calls, cash advance fees, and "hardship" withdrawals. And, in case you get turned down for a loan, you'll find advice about boosting your chances on your next application. You'll even discover whether you can deduct the interest paid on a loan on your taxes this year. Finally, you'll learn what to do if you can't make your monthly loan repayments.

CONVENTIONS USED IN THIS BOOK

You'll find the following icons used throughout this book to help you understand technical terms and to highlight hidden dangers and helpful shortcuts:

 Timesaver Tip icons offer ideas that save time and eliminate confusion.

 Plain English icons define new and complicated terms.

 Panic Button icons identify potential problems and how to solve them.

ACKNOWLEDGMENTS

Warmest thanks to all who contributed to the research needed for this book, especially European American Bank, Scudder, Stevens & Clark, American Express Financial Advisors, HSH Associates, the American Council of Life Insurance, Jackie Clark, Randall McCathren, Mark Kutz, Bill Mauldin—and to Bob Wagner, the best title insurance man in the business.

THE AUTHOR

Barbara Hetzer is a journalist who writes frequently about business and personal finance issues. Her work has appeared in numerous publications, including *Business Week, Advertising Age, Fortune, Self, Working Woman, Business Month, First for Women*, and *Cosmopolitan*.

WHAT IS SMART BOROWING?

In this lesson, you'll learn why you should borrow money to invest in a home, stocks, bonds, and other assets, and how to pick those assets wisely.

THE RIGHT KIND OF DEBT

Despite what your mother may have told you, you won't get rich by saving your pennies. Nine times out of ten, you'll find that wealthy people built their fortunes using *other people's money*. In other words, they *borrowed* it.

Too much debt, of course, is no good for anyone's balance sheet. Still, like most consumers, you will fare better financially if you begin to think "smarter" about borrowing money.

Naturally, it doesn't make sense to borrow money carelessly. Putting one purchase after another onto a credit card that charges 17.5% interest—and then paying just the minimum balance every month—is like throwing away your money. You're simply borrowing money to *spend*. That's almost always a bad idea.

But borrowing money to *invest*...Now that's a "smart" way to think about your finances. Whether it's a new home, law school for your daughter, or a hot stock you can't wait to get your hands on, you're not just spending money; you're investing in an *asset*. And, ultimately, that's how you amass wealth—by building assets with investment debt.

Asset An asset is property owned by an individual or a corporation. Basically, it's everything that you own, such as a house, a car, stocks and bonds, and money in the bank. *Net assets* are what's left over after you've subtracted all of your debts.

Investment Debt Investment debt is money that you borrow to buy an asset, like a house. Ultimately, if you choose the asset wisely—and have a bit of luck, too—your investment will rise in value and yield a profit when you sell it.

Of course, you may borrow money to buy an asset like a house, which may not yield a profit. Does that mean you've failed financially? No. While you may not have quadrupled your investment, you have, enjoyed a comfortable home to live in—and a nice tax deduction, too.

Perhaps you plan to borrow money to buy a car. You've heard, no doubt, that a car's resale value drops precipitously the instant you drive it out of the showroom. So what? In the long run, it may be cheaper to *invest* in a new car than to repair your old jalopy yet again.

Crucial Test The money that you borrow shouldn't just disappear. That means, you shouldn't borrow to take a two-week jaunt to Tahiti or to foot the bill for a seven-course dinner at the swankiest restaurant in town. Remember, your ultimate goal is to increase your assets.

CHOOSE YOUR ASSETS WISELY

The dizzying array of investment opportunities available today can make your head spin. You can now invest in nearly anything, from the basic starter home to a real estate investment trust, from gold and silver to blue chip stocks, or from diamonds and gems to vintage Barbie dolls. Unfortunately, there's no one perfect investment. Nor is there one sure-fire way to invest.

First, acquaint yourself with some of the major investment possibilities on the following pages. Then, figure out what your financial goals are and how much debt you can handle. (You'll learn about debt in the next lesson.)

These answers will narrow your investment choices considerably. Finally, decide where your investment funds will come from.

INVESTING IN REAL ESTATE

Whether it's a house, a condo, or a co-op, the purchase of a home is probably the single biggest investment that you'll ever make. Unfortunately, in the last decade and a half you've probably seen that real estate doesn't always go up. While it's not the "safe bet" investment it once was, over the long run the value of most homes should keep pace with inflation.

INVESTING IN MUTUAL FUNDS

To invest in mutual funds, individuals pool their money into a large fund managed by investment professionals. Rather than buying just one or two stocks or bonds, you buy shares in a variety of companies and institutions.

Almost everyone loves mutual funds. Why? They offer professional money-management, which is especially helpful if you're not an experienced investor. Funds charge very low fees, if any at all, and don't require an exorbitant initial investment. Mutual funds can be as risky or as safe an investment as you choose. With some 7,000 funds to choose from, you're sure to find a fund that matches your investment "style." For instance, if you want a high return, invest in an aggressive growth fund. Because these investments fluctuate widely from month to month, it's a much riskier investment than, say, a balanced fund, which invests in both stocks and bonds.

INVESTING IN STOCKS

When you invest in a stock, you buy a share of ownership in the corporation that is issuing the stock. The two types of stock are *common* and *preferred*. Preferred stock owners receive a fixed dividend rate (a cash payment made to stockholders that represents a share of the company's profits), set at the time the shares are issued. Dividends paid to common stock owners fluctuate, depending upon how much profit the company generates that year. Preferred stock owners do not get voting rights as common stock owners do.

Investing in stocks can be risky—especially if you don't know what you're doing—but over time, no other investment performs better. The return on stocks has consistently been about 7% higher than inflation over the last 25 years or so. There's no absolutely safe way to play the market, of course. But if you do some research, spread your investment money among several stocks instead of just one, and don't pay attention to day-to-day fluctuations in prices, you should come out ahead.

INVESTING IN BONDS

When a company or the government issues a bond, they are basically writing an IOU to raise money. You lend money to the issuer—by making an investment in a bond—and are re-paid, with interest, when the bond matures at a later date.

Bonds come in three basic types:

- Treasury: issued by the federal government
- Corporate: issued by corporations
- Tax-Exempt Municipals: issued by states, cities, and other municipalities

You probably assume that bonds are a safe, secure investment. If you're talking about U.S. EE savings bonds, this is true. However, non-government issued bonds are often subject to some of the same ups and downs as stocks. As a rule, the longer the length of maturity of the bond, the higher the rate of return. Therefore, bonds are best purchased as long-term investments.

 The Rule of Bonds Bonds have an inverse relationship with interest rates. When interest rates rise, bond prices fall—and you, the investor, lose money.

INVESTING IN COMMODITIES

Commodities are tangible investments, like gold and silver, and agricultural products, such as cocoa beans, wheat, soybeans, and pork bellies (just a fancy name for bacon). Investors generally buy *commodities futures*, not the commodity itself.

 Commodities Futures With commodities futures, you contract to buy or sell a commodity within a certain period of time. Basically, you're betting that the price of wheat, let's say, will rise or fall on a specific date.

This is a fast-paced, risky investment arena because politics, droughts, or general business announcements—virtually anything—can cause the price of commodities to swing wildly. Don't invest in commodities because you think you're going to make a killing overnight. That's not likely to happen.

 A Loser's Game An estimated 75% of speculators lose money in the commodities market. Unfortunately, it's the experts and insiders who generally reap the big gains.

INVESTING IN "COLLECTIBLES"

Be it antique books, Art Deco jewelry, vintage cars, or your grandmother's favorite china, somebody, somewhere probably collects it. Some items are worth only a few dollars. Others are valued at hundreds of thousands of dollars.

Most people collect things because they love the objects themselves, so this isn't a purely financial investment. In fact, some collectors get so caught up in the joys of the hobby itself—talking with other collectors, hunting for finds at estate sales—that they often forget about the supposed monetary gains.

That's the downside to collectibles. Collectibles are also risky because their value rises and falls so quickly. Public taste is extremely capricious; what's hotly pursued today may be old news tomorrow.

 Anticipate Trends Once a collectible becomes popular, it's too late to start collecting for investment.

In this lesson, you learned why you should borrow money to invest in assets and how to choose those assets wisely. In the next lesson, you will learn how to calculate your net worth, draw up a financial plan, and determine how much debt you can handle.

CHECK YOUR FINANCIAL HEALTH

In this lesson, you'll learn how to calculate your net worth, draw up a financial plan, and determine the amount of debt that you can handle comfortably.

CHECK YOUR FINANCIAL FITNESS

Before borrowing money to make any kind of investment, it's smart to check your financial fitness. How much money do you have available, for instance? What's your current debt load? How are your other investments doing? Are you still saving? If so, how much? And for what, exactly?

To answer these questions and more, start by listing your financial goals. Since everyone has their own needs and desires, there's no one right answer. You may want to buy a big-screen T.V. Your neighbors may want to send their children to an Ivy League college.

All of these goals carry different price tags. Some of your goals will probably change from year to year, maybe even from month to month. The key: keep your goals clearly defined.

To determine your goals, you may want to organize them as follows:

- **Short-Term Goals.** You can usually achieve these in a year or less. Examples: Saving for a vacation to Bermuda or a new CD-ROM drive for your computer.

- **Mid-Term Goals.** You'll need a heftier chunk of change to attain this wish-list. Think of these as your basic "5-year plans." Examples: Saving for a down payment on a house or to remodel the kitchen.

- **Long-Term Goals.** These require a substantial amount of money—saved *over time*—and lots of planning. Examples: Saving for your retirement nest egg or your children's college education.

CALCULATING YOUR NET WORTH

Once you've established where you want to go, your next step is to determine where you are right now—your starting point, basically. That's called your net worth.

 Net Worth   Net worth is your assets minus your liabilities. It's the money you would have left over after selling all of your possessions and paying off your debts.

To find your net worth, first add up the value of all your assets. These can include: cash and bank account balances; stocks, bonds, and certificates of deposit; shares in mutual funds; cash value of life insurance policies, art, jewelry, and other collections, as well as other personal belongings, like a car and furnishings; equity in a home or business; and value of your 401(k) or other retirement plan.

Now, subtract everything that you owe (your liabilities). This can include: any real estate mortgages; the outstanding balances of any home equity, auto, college, or other loans; and the amount you owe on credit cards.

The remainder is your net worth. Ideally, you should have a surplus of assets—the larger the better.

Zero—Or Less You may find that you *owe* more than you *own*. Don't worry if you're a homeowner with an outstanding mortgage, or if you're a college grad with student loans (especially if you have a job). Do worry, however, if most of that debt is loaded on a high-interest rate credit card.

Net worth figures can be misleading because a good chunk of your assets are not really usable. You'll pay a penalty, for instance, if you tap into most retirement plans before age 59 1/2 or if you cash in a certificate of deposit before it has matured.

When analyzing your portfolio (or holdings), make sure that you strike a balance between assets that are tied up, such as your house, and *liquid assets* that can be turned into cash quickly, such as mutual funds, stocks, and bonds.

Emergency Fund Keep three to six months of living expenses available in a liquid asset. You can then tap into these funds in case of an emergency, like a job loss or an accident.

DRAWING UP A FINANCIAL PLAN

Obviously, you want your net worth to increase year after year. But that's not as easy as it sounds. Like most people, you probably have no idea where your money goes. You know you spend money on take-out food, gas, and toys for the kids, but you don't know *how much* you spend.

To meet your financial goals, you need a good, solid budget to keep you on track. If a budget sounds too much like a diet— and you can't stick to either one—then call it a spending plan. The idea is to think of your household as a business. And, like any business, you want it to generate a profit.

 Most Popular Timetable You can draw up a budget for whatever time period you like—monthly, quarterly, or yearly. Most people find the monthly budget easiest to manage.

It's time to sharpen your pencils and get down to the nitty-gritty. Your budget worksheet should begin with your monthly income. From that figure, subtract any pre-tax contributions for a retirement fund, medical benefits, or the like. Then subtract FICA and income taxes. The final sum will be your take-home pay. (See Table 2.1.)

TABLE 2.1   CALCULATING YOUR TAKE-HOME PAY

Monthly income	$3,400
401(k) contribution	- 444
FICA/income taxes	- 790
Take-home pay	$2,166

Next, list your expenses and fill in the amount you spend each month. (To get an accurate picture, check your receipts for the last several months.) Make your categories as specific as possible. Instead of lumping all of your entertainment expenses together, for instance, divide them up into separate categories such as books, magazine subscriptions, health club membership, video rentals, and so on.

Don't forget your debt—the outstanding balance on your credit card is an expense, too—or that cup of coffee you buy on your way into the office every day. Those little expenditures really add up. (See Table 2.2.)

TABLE 2.2   EXPENSES, FROM A SAMPLE BUDGET

HOUSEHOLD

Groceries _____

Laundry/Dry Cleaning _____

Rent/Mortgage & Property Taxes & Insurance _____

Repairs/Service Calls _____

Utilities:

Electricity _____

Heat/Fuel _____

Telephone _____

Water _____

PERSONAL

Books _____

Clothing _____

Transportation To Work _____

PERSONAL

Cosmetics _____

Lunch _____

Miscellaneous Entertainment _____

Subscriptions _____

Video Rentals _____

Dinners Out _____

Music _____

KIDS

Allowance _____

Childcare _____

Clothing _____

Lunch Money _____

Tuition _____

TRANSPORTATION

Car _____

Public _____

INSURANCE

Auto _____

Disability _____

Homeowner's _____

Life _____

Medical/Dental _____

continues

TABLE 2.2   CONTINUED

MISCELLANEOUS EXPENSES

Charitable Contributions   _____

Dues   _____

Gifts   _____

Morning Coffee and Danish   _____

Pets   _____

Vacation   _____

DEBT PAYMENTS (OTHER THAN MORTGAGE)

Auto Loan   _____

Credit Card Balance   _____

Installment Payments (on furniture) _____

Personal Loan   _____

Finally, subtract your expenses from your monthly take-home pay. This is the money available for savings and/or investment. (See Table 2.3.)

TABLE 2.3   MONEY AVAILABLE FOR INVESTMENT

Monthly Take-Home Pay	$2,166
Monthly Expenses	- 1,700
Money Available	$466

HOW MUCH DEBT CAN YOU HANDLE?

Most experts agree that up to 35% of your earnings can be allotted to monthly debt repayments (including mortgage repayments). If you don't have a mortgage (or an education or business loan), however, your consumer debt should not exceed 20% of your take-home pay.

Five Sure-Fire Signs that You're Too Deep in Debt:

1. You use cash advances from one credit card to pay the balance on your other credit card.
2. You don't know how much you owe.
3. Collection agencies call you regularly.
4. You pay all your bills late.
5. You have trouble sleeping at night because you're worried that you can't pay your bills.

 A Safe Bet   When you borrow money to make an investment, you can easily afford that debt if it supports itself. Let's say you invest in some real estate—a condo, for example. Can you rent the condo for more than the mortgage is costing you? If so, then it's a good deal.

In this lesson, you learned how to calculate your net worth, draw up a financial plan, and determine the amount of debt that you can handle comfortably. In the next lesson, you will learn how to pick a lender and how to negotiate a loan.

PICKING A LENDER

In this lesson, you'll learn how to pick a lender and how to negotiate the best deal on a loan.

THE BEST WAYS TO DEAL WITH LENDING INSTITUTIONS

You may be overwhelmed at the prospect of going to a bank or other lending institution to get a loan. You may worry that you'll be turned down because you're not rich enough or well-connected.

Banks don't give loans for free. They charge you big bucks—interest—to borrow their money. Banks want your business, especially if your credit is good. And they're often willing to bend over backwards to sign you up.

So start thinking like a customer—instead of someone begging for a handout. Like any other purchase, you should shop around first to see what's out there. Does this bank offer a product that best suits your needs? Do you really want all those extra options? Have you found the best price?

More Clout   Some lenders have a policy called "cross-selling." If you already have a checking or savings account at a particular lending institution, they might offer you a better rate on a loan.

Banks aren't the only places you can borrow money. Nor do all banks offer the same array of products and services. In general, smaller institutions charge lower interest rates and fewer fees than larger ones. And most lenders are regulated, to some extent, by state and/or federal government agencies.

Rating Service   Call Veribanc, a rating service in Wakefield, Massachusetts (800-442-2657), to check out your lender's health. For $10, Veribanc will rate the financial soundness of any bank, savings and loan, or credit union. (It'll cost you $5 for each additional institution.) Three stars and "green" is best, while no stars and "red" is the worst.

Troubled Lenders   If you're *borrowing* money, it doesn't usually matter how healthy the institution is because you already have your money in hand. What's the worst thing that could happen? The bank goes bust—and your loan is payable to somebody else. However, if you're thinking about using a home equity line and your lender goes under, the government could cancel the unused portion of your credit line. And that might put you in a bind, especially if you really need the cash and have to start searching for another loan elsewhere.

THE CREDIT UNION

Another popular source of loans are credit unions. These are non-profit institutions generally composed of employees and their families, who deposit savings and can borrow against those savings to finance a purchase such as a car or a house. Many large companies, schools, and even government agencies have credit unions these days.

Usually, credit unions offer very low rates—lower than those of most banks. You'll have no trouble getting a loan if you're a member in good standing. In fact, that's the biggest obstacle. You *must* be a member or related to someone who is.

And just how do you join a credit union? Check with your employer's benefits office first. If you belong to a professional organization or club, that may enable you to join, too. There are even some credit unions organized by ethnicity (i.e., the Polish-American Credit Union) and geographic location (i.e., the Bethpage Federal Credit Union). If you still can't find a group to join, contact the Credit Union National Association in Madison, Wisconsin (800-358-5710), for details about other credit unions that you might be eligible to join.

Not Enough Insurance   Make sure that your credit union is a member of the Federal Deposit Insurance Corporation (FDIC), which guarantees that deposits of up to $100,000 will be safe even if the credit union fails. Not all credit unions have this.

The Bank

Once the only lenders of mortgage money, *savings banks* (and savings & loan associations) still account for the majority of home loans. Generally, you can borrow money fairly easily if your credit is good, and you'll often find better, more personal service here than at a large commercial bank. (Costs are frequently lower, too, especially for home improvement and personal loans.)

While *commercial banks* once provided loans only to businesses, they now deal with individuals, also. They're very convenient because there are lots of branches and they offer a wide range of products—from personal loans to auto loans to business loans.

However, because of their size, commercial banks are often impersonal. As a result, some commercial banks have created "private banking" divisions that offer more personalized service. Unfortunately, these services are usually available to the more affluent customers.

 Who's Who?   If you can't figure out if it's a commercial bank or an S&L (Savings and Loan), look for "National Bank" or "Bank, N.A.," in the name. That means it's a commecial bank. Most savings banks use the word "savings" somewhere in their name.

The Consumer Finance Company

Often referred to as "hard money" lenders, consumer finance companies generally charge higher interest rates and higher fees than anyone else. Why? Because if you need money quickly or you can't get money anyplace else, they'll usually give it to you here—even if your credit rating is poor. Names that may sound familiar include: Household Finance, GMAC Credit Corp., GE Capital Credit Corp., The Money Store, and Oxford Credit Group.

Worth a Look Consumer finance companies have recently jumped on the home-equity bandwagon. Their rates are competitive with many banks.

THE MORTGAGE COMPANY

Mortgage companies have only one business—mortgages, first- and second-mortgages, as well as home equity lines—so you can usually find very attractive deals through mortgage companies.

You'll want to consult a mortgage company if you're looking for a government-backed loan or your situation is somewhat atypical. These lenders specialize in "no-income verification" loans, for instance, which require just a quick check of your income and employment. This arrangement is particularly advantageous if you're self-employed.

What's in a Name? Don't confuse mortgage companies with mortgage *brokers*. The latter shop for a mortgage for you. Generally, it doesn't cost any more to borrow through a mortgage broker than to deal with a lender directly.

The Federal Government

Uncle Sam can help you out—especially if you need money to buy a house. If you qualify, you can get a mortgage backed by the:

- Federal Housing Administration (FHA)
- Federal National Mortgage Association (Fannie Mae)
- Federal Home Loan Mortgage Corp. (Freddie Mac)
- Department of Veterans Affairs (VA)

Most states also operate their own mortgage agencies, such as the State of New York Mortgage Association (Sonny Mae) and the Connecticut Housing Finance Authority (CHFA).

As a consumer, you can't seek a loan from a government agency directly. You must apply for these loans through a mortgage bank, or a commercial or savings bank. (Not every lender offers these mortgages either.) The requirements vary, but often these mortgages offer lower-than-average interest rates and require a smaller down payment. The downside? There's a limit to how much you can borrow.

Negotiating the Best Deal

If you were buying a new car, you would never just walk in off the street and pay the sticker price. The same theory applies when you're shopping for a loan. Comparison-shop at a handful of the above-mentioned lenders. That means more than just finding out the interest rate. Ask about additional fees, prepayment penalties, and the length of the loan. Then compare notes—and get ready to negotiate.

If Bank Across the Street has a higher interest rate—but better service and a more convenient location—than Bank Around the World, tell Bank Across the Street. Maybe it will be willing to meet its competitor's price. Another tactic is to tell the lender how much cash you need, and why. (The reason is important: Auto loans, for example, cost more than personal loans.) Then ask for the lender's best offer.

To make a mortgage, a lender will probably charge you one to three points. A *point* is a fee that the lender charges the borrower to arrange the mortgage. One point equals one percent of the total loan amount. Also called loan origination fees, maximum loan charges, loan discounts, or discount points, points are almost always negotiable. You can usually "buy down" your interest rate, in fact, by paying more points up front. Or, you can pay fewer points and get a higher interest rate on the loan.

Points vs. Interest   So which is better—more points or a lower interest rate? That depends upon how long you plan on staying in the house. Generally, if you're settling in for more than five years, pay the extra points to get the lowest-possible mortgage interest rate.

To finalize the mortgage loan process, you'll attend a *closing* at the bank or an attorney's office. Here, the mortgage documents are reviewed and signed, and any last-minute negotiations are haggled over. Finally, the lender hands you a check for the loan amount (which you then give to the seller). In return, you the get the deed to the house, and the keys to the front door. (That means, the house is yours!) If you're applying for a home-equity loan, the bank will hand you a check at the closing (and you get to keep it).

You may have an attorney represent you, but it's not necessary. In addition to points, some other fees that you may have to pay at closing include:

- **Legal Fees.** Not just yours, but those of your lender.

- **Title Insurance.** The lender wants to know if there are any liens against the property.

- **Document Preparation.** The typical cost to record a document is $7 to $14 per document.

- **Appraisal Fee.** Is your house worth more than the amount you want to borrow?

- **Credit Check.** How much money do you owe to other lenders? Do you pay your bills on time? Have you ever declared bankruptcy?

- **Application Fees.** The lender charges you a fee to process the loan application.

- **Inspection.** The lender wants to know that the home isn't infested with termites.

In most cases, a closing could cost you anywhere between $500 and $5,000.

In this lesson, you learned how to pick a lender and how to negotiate the best deal on a loan. In the next lesson, you will learn how much money you can borrow to invest in a house.

4

INVESTING IN A HOUSE

In this lesson, you'll learn how much money you can borrow to invest in a house.

IS HOME OWNERSHIP AN INVESTOR'S DREAM?

Owning your own home is the American Dream. For a time, it seemed to be the investor's dream, too. In the early 80s, consumers were earning double-digit returns on homes that they had purchased less than five years earlier.

Now homes will hopefully keep pace with inflation. But it's safe to assume, unfortunately, that those stellar investment days of home ownership are gone forever.

Buying a home, however, is still the single biggest investment that most of you will make. But most people don't generally buy homes purely for financial reasons. You buy a home because it's a nice place to live and raise a family—and you don't have to deal with a difficult landlord or a noisy tenant upstairs.

In addition, mortgage payments are tax-deductible and enable you to build equity (ownership) in an asset. (That's money you might not have saved otherwise.) And at some very, very distant point in the future, you'll live mortgage-free.

How Much Can You Borrow?

A mortgage is like any other loan, except for one important difference. If you default on the mortgage (you don't make your payments), the lender must take you to court (a time-consuming process known as foreclosure) to get the property back. That's why it's usually much more complicated to get a mortgage than a car loan. Principal is the dollar amount of the original loan, on which you pay interest. Mortgage payments consist of principal and interest.

Once you've decided that you want to invest in a home, you must figure out how large a mortgage you can afford. This will determine the price of the home you can buy.

Lenders will give you a mortgage based solely upon your income and how much debt you owe. (Sometimes they will consider your other assets, too.) The most commonly used criteria for issuing loans is called the "28/36" ratio. It has two parts. Here's how it works:

1. No more than *28%* of your gross monthly income (that's before taxes) should be used to repay the principal and interest on your mortgage.

2. The total amount of debt that you have—that's your mortgage *and* consumer debt, like auto loans and student loans—should not exceed *36%* of your gross monthly income. Generally, that "total" includes any debts that will take at least ten more months to pay off. Credit card debt usually isn't included—unless you have a lot of high balances.

Calculate your monthly principal and interest (P&I) payment, using the equation in Table 4.1. This will give you a rough estimate of the amount that you can afford to spend on housing each month. For an even better estimate, add in mortgage taxes and insurance (if those numbers are readily available at this stage).

TABLE 4.1   EASY CALCULATION OF P&I*

$4,500 (Your Monthly Gross Income)
× .28

$1,260 (Your Maximum P&I Payment)

Source: HSH Associates, Butler, NJ

Next, find that estimated maximum P&I payment in the chart below (Table 4.2) to see how much you can borrow at a few typical rates.

TABLE 4.2   HOW MUCH CAN YOU BORROW?*

RATE	P&I: $1000/MO.		P&I: $1250/MO.		P&I: $1500/MO.		P&I: $1750/MO.	
6.5	114.7	158.2	143.4	197.7	172.1	237.3	200.8	276.8
7.5	107.8	143.0	134.8	178.7	161.8	214.5	188.7	250.2
8.0	104.6	136.2	130.8	170.3	156.9	204.4	183.1	238.4
8.5	101.5	130.0	126.9	162.5	152.3	195.0	177.7	227.5
TERM	15 YR	30 YR	15 YR	30 YR	15 YR	30 YR	15 YR	30 YR

Source: HSH Associates, Butler, NJ

Select an interest rate. Obviously you'll have to do your homework here. Check the newspapers or ask your realtor or lender what the average current interest rate is. Let's assume it's 8%. If your maximum P&I is $1250, then you can borrow up to $170,000.

LARGE VS. SMALL DOWN PAYMENT

In addition to deciding what size mortgage you need, you have to make sure that you have enough money for a down payment. A *down payment* refers to a percentage of the purchase price of the house that you pay up front. Generally, this amount isn't taken from the mortgage loan because down payments, as a rule, can't be borrowed money.

The minimum down payment is usually 5% of the selling price. This means, on a $200,000 house, your down payment would equal $10,000. The most common down payment is 20%. If you put down less than that, you generally must pay Private Mortgage Insurance (PMI), which will add another 0.25% to your interest rate. Why? Because if you default on your loan, the bank won't get all of its money back. Your down payment was so small that there's little, if any, equity in the house. And, although the bank would foreclose on the house, such proceedings rarely garner the full value of the house.

More Mortgage Insurance Don't confuse private mortgage insurance—which protects the bank in case you default on your mortgage—with *mortgage insurance*, which protects you. When you buy the latter, your mortgage gets paid off when you die.

The more money that you initially put down, the smaller the loan you'll have to borrow, and the lower your mortgage payments will be each month. You want to get the lowest monthly payment possible if you're close to retirement or if you're on a fixed income and you don't expect your income to rise in the near future.

Large down payments make less sense if it means you're spending every last penny. You still need some cash on hand for unanticipated expenses or emergencies. In theory, you can always tap into those funds via a home equity line, but it's not as liquid as money in the bank.

 No Down Payment! If you're a current or former G.I., you can get a mortgage backed by the Department of Veterans Affairs that offers 100% financing. Other government-backed mortgages offer even sweeter deals. In some cases, you can get financing for the entire purchase price, plus closing costs.

SHORT-TERM VS. LONG-TERM MORTGAGES

Not too long ago, almost everyone got a 30-year mortgage. Now, the length of the *mortgage term* (how long you borrow the money) is another option that you must choose. There are dozens of variations. Most lenders offer terms of 15, 30, and even 40 years. Generally, a longer term loan will have lower monthly payments, but it'll cost you much more in interest over the life of the loan.

 Interest Payments Add Up With a 30-year mortgage, you repay more than three times the amount you borrow over the life of the loan.

For instance, a 15-year mortgage will build equity faster than a 30-year mortgage. And you'll often get a better deal from the lender; interest rates on a 15-year term are often as much as a half-percentage point lower than on 30-year mortgages. Plus, you'll save more than $100,000 in interest payments. (See Table 4.3.)

TABLE 4.3 COMPARING TERMS ON A **$100,000** MORTGAGE*
15-year vs. 30-year vs. 40-year mortgage   (The interst rate is 10%)

MORTGAGE TERM	MONTHLY PAYMENT	TOTAL INTEREST PAID OVER LIFE OF LOAN
15-Year	$1,075	$93,429
30-Year	$878	$215,926
40-Year	$849	$307,590

Source: HSH Associates, Butler, NJ

Just Out of Reach   Monthly payments on a 15-year mortgage are not twice those of a 30-year mortgage. Generally, they're just about 20% higher. That's not so much really—until you consider that you need 20% more income to qualify for a 15-year mortgage.

Don't Do It   40-year mortgages are seldom a smart choice. On a $100,000 mortgage (Table 4.3), the difference in payments between a 30-year and 40-year loan is a mere $29 per month. Yet you'll pay almost $100,000 more in interest over the life of the loan. If you can't afford the payments of a 30-year mortgage, you probably can't afford to buy a home.

First-time home buyers often choose a 30-year mortgage because the lower payments seem more manageable. After a year
or so of making their monthly payments rather easily, however, you may regret selecting such a long-term loan because
you're paying so much in interest.

You don't have to refinance. You can get the lower-interest
benefits of a 15-year mortgage simply by making one extra
monthly mortgage payment per year. The result: You'll pay off
a 30-year mortgage in roughly 18 years. Just be sure to tell the
lender that you want the extra amount applied to the loan
principal. (Make sure that your mortgage doesn't carry any
prepayment penalities, too.)

Not for Everybody   Even if you can manage the
steeper payments of a 15-year loan—or make that
extra monthly payment on a 30-year term—you
may not want to. You could always plunk that extra
cash into another more lucrative investment.

In this lesson, you learned how much money you can borrow
to invest in a house. In the next lesson, you will learn how to
choose between a fixed-rate mortgage and an adjustable-rate
mortgage.

5

FINDING THE RIGHT MORTGAGE

In this lesson, you'll learn how to choose between a fixed-rate mortgage and an adjustable-rate mortgage.

NAVIGATING THE MORTGAGE MAZE

It used to be so easy. Home-buyers searched until they found that perfect center-hall colonial and then took out a 30-year, fixed-rate mortgage to pay for it. Today, buyers must wander through a maze of complicated mortgage choices. Do you want an adjustable-rate with an option to convert or the fixed-rate with graduated payments?

All those rates and terms can be so confusing, especially when you consider that picking the wrong mortgage could cost you plenty. You can save hundreds of thousands of dollars in interest payments by choosing a 15-year fixed-rate mortgage over a 30-year adjustable-rate mortgage. But that doesn't necessarily mean that's the right choice for you.

Before you sign on the dotted line, make sure you understand what options you're getting and how much the mortgage really costs. By learning the basics, you'll be able to find the mortgage that's right for you.

FIXED-RATE MORTGAGES

Still one of the most popular types of mortgages, a fixed-rate mortgage features a *fixed* interest rate, generally with a term of 15 or 30 years. With this type of mortgage, you lock in an interest rate, either when your application is approved or at the closing. Even if rates rise in subsequent years, your interest rate stays the same—forever. Your monthly payment will never change over the life of the loan.

Mortgages guaranteed by the federal government, such as a Federal Housing Administration (FHA) loan, usually allow low- to middle-income folks (who don't make enough money to qualify for a more traditional mortgage) to make a modest down payment and borrow money at a lower interest rate than similar fixed-rate loans. To qualify in most areas, you can't borrow more than $155,250.

 Best Buy   If they qualify, most home-buyers opt for a fixed-rate loan when interest rates start falling below 10%.

Fixed-rate loans offer several variations. Some features, like "graduated payment," may help you qualify for a fixed-rate loan. During the first few years, payments are lower because you don't pay all of the interest that is due. Eventually, your payments increase—typically by 5% to 7.5% per year—until your payments include all of the interest due.

Negative Amortization   Because you're defer-
ring interest, known as *negative amortization*, a
graduated-payment loan actually gets bigger
rather than smaller in the early life of the loan. The
drawback? If you sell your house within a few
years, you may find that you owe even more than
you originally borrowed.

Other fixed-rate loan variations can save you a substantial
amount in interest payments—yet still offer a comfortable fixed
interest rate. A *bi-weekly payment* schedule, for instance, will pay
off your mortgage faster. Generally, a mortgage is paid monthly,
but under a bi-weekly arrangement, you'll pay one half of your
monthly payment every two weeks. So what? By year-end,
you'll have made thirteen payments per year, instead of twelve.

 When Rates Go Down   A fixed interest rate
means you're locked in for life. However, if interest
rates drop significantly, you can always refinance
at a lower rate.

 Annual Percentage Rate   To compare the cost
of one fixed-rate loan to another, look at the annual
percentage rate (APR) rather than just the interest
rate. The APR is higher than the stated interest
rate because it includes points and other upfront fees,
but it reflects the *actual* cost of your loan.

Fixed-rate mortgages are a good choice for you if:

- You live on a fixed income.
- Interest rates are low.
- You like the security of knowing that your monthly payments will not change.
- You can't afford higher monthly payments.

ADJUSTABLE-RATE MORTGAGES (ARMs)

An ARM features an *adjustable* interest rate. Unlike a fixed-rate mortgage, this rate can change (or *adjust*) periodically—typically every year or six months. This means that your monthly payment will change, too. If rates rise, you'll probably pay a heftier payment each month. If rates fall, you'll pay less. Initially, these interest rates start out much lower than fixed rates. On a $100,000 mortgage, for example, a two-point differential can mean savings of more than $140 per month. (See Table 5.1.)

TABLE 5.1   WORST-CASE SCENARIO
ADJUSTABLE-RATE VS. FIXED-RATE ON $100,000 LOAN*

YEAR	TYPE	RATE	MONTHLY P&I
1	30-yr. FR	7%	$ 665.35
	ARM	4.125%	$ 484.65
2	30-yr. FR	7%	$ 665.35
	ARM	6.125%	$ 604.39
3	30-yr. FR	6.125%	$ 665.35
	ARM	8.125%	$ 732.73
4	30-yr. FR	6.125%	$ 665.35
	ARM	10.125%	$ 867.55
5	30-yr. FR	6.125%	$ 665.35
	ARM	10.125%	$ 867.55

Source: HSH Associates, Butler, NJ

ARMs are attractive because their initial lower rates—and, thus, lower monthly payments—allow many homeowners to qualify for the loan. It's usually easier, in fact, to qualify for an ARM than for a fixed-rate loan.

The rules for qualifying for an ARM have recently changed. If you put less than 20% down, many lenders won't grant you an ARM—unless you show that you can afford not only the initial lower payments *but* the increased payments thereafter.

Your ARM rate is tied to an *index*, which is a known benchmark used by a lender to set its mortgage rate on an adjustable-rate loan. The two most popular indexes are one-year Treasury bills and the 11th District Cost of Funds, which tracks Savings & Loan funds in California, Arizona, and Nevada. When the index goes up, or down, the lender adjusts the homeowner's rate accordingly. Generally, a lender offers a low introductory rate for the first year. During the second year, however, the ARM rate zooms up to the index rate—plus a margin that the lender tacks on. Your ARM rate will continue to rise—or fall—with the index.

Teasers   Teasers are initial ARM rates that are extra low because they're meant to reel you in. They may, or may not, be good deals. Find out what the rate will be after the first adjustment, and how frequently the rate adjusts. Generally, the more often the rate changes, the lower your initial interest rate.

Like fixed-rate mortgages, ARMs offer a variety of features and options. One popular feature does not adjust the rate for three years. In other words, your initial rate and payment are frozen at that introductory rate—much like a fixed-rate loan—for three years. Then, it's subject to the same rise and fall of other ARM rates.

The most popular variation is the *convertible ARM*. This enables you to convert the loan to a fixed-rate mortgage within five years. In most cases, you'll pay a one-time fee of a few hundred dollars to convert the loan. And you'll get a rate that is slightly higher than the going-rate for fixed-rate mortgages. Generally, converting costs far less than refinancing the loan, which may cost as much as 5 to 6 percent of the total amount you're borrowing. Keep in mind, however, that some lenders charge up-front fees just for the *option* to convert your adjustable-rate mortgage to a fixed-rate mortgage.

 Win-Win Rate   A *convertible ARM* is ideal for the home buyer who doesn't qualify for a fixed-rate mortgage, but wants one. You can take advantage of the low starter rate, and then convert to a stable rate when fixed-rates fall.

Many ARMs offer a "cap" that limits how much the interest rate can rise each year and over the life of the loan. For example: A good ARM rate won't rise more than 2% per year, or 6% over the life of the loan. (See Table 5.1.)

 More Negative Amortization   In some ARMs, the payment is adjusted annually, but the rate changes *monthly*. That could lead to negative amortization: the loan balance may increase if your monthly payments don't rise as fast as the interest rate.

Adjustable-rate mortgages are a good choice for you if:

1. You need the lower rate and lower monthly payments to qualify for the loan you need.

2. You're a first-time home buyer and you expect your income to rise in the next few years.

3. You plan on selling your home in five years or less.

4. Fixed interest rates are high and you expect them to be lower in the next few years.

Quick Roundup   To find the best mortgage deals in your area, order HSH Associates' Homebuyer's Mortgage Kit (800-873-2837; $20), which reports on up to 80 lenders, depending on the area covered. You'll receive data about the interest rate, points, application fees, and other fees charged by each lender. Best of all, this mortgage information is updated weekly.

In this lesson, you learned how to choose between a fixed-rate mortgage and an adjustable-rate mortgage. In the next lesson, you will learn how to invest in a second home, co-op, or condo.

6

Buying a
Second Home

*In this lesson, you'll learn how to buy a vacation home and a
condo.*

The Second Home Market

Be it a beachfront condo in Malibu, a rustic cabin deep in the
woods of Vermont, or the luxury suite of a ski chalet in Vail,
owning a second home seems like Paradise. But is it a good
investment?

Markets for vacation homes have suffered the same fate as the
regular housing market. There's a glut of properties, and prices
are still down substantially from their early 80s peak.

Like a first home, a second home forces you to save—and gives
you substantial borrowing power. Renters, year-round or sea-
sonal, can always help you pay expenses. Plus, you have a nice
place to spend your two weeks off every year.

But a vacation home isn't a true investment. Sure, the house
might make money eventually—if property values have risen
enough by the time you sell it. Most likely, you'd get a better

yield investing your dollars elsewhere. Keep in mind that vacation homes should be bought primarily for fun, not substantial profit.

FINANCING, RENTING, AND OTHER FACTS ABOUT VACATION HOMES

Second homes can be expensive. You'll have to pay another mortgage, another set of taxes, another insurance, as well as utilities and maintenance.

By law, you can claim only one primary residence. So even if you never plan on renting your vacation home to anyone, you'll still have to apply for a "non-owner occupied" mortgage. And that generally costs more than a loan for a first home. Expect to pay a higher interest rate, extra points, and/or a heftier down payment, too. Not all lenders grant loans for second homes either, so you'll have to shop around.

 Buyer Beware   A first home isn't exactly a *liquid* investment, but vacation homes are definitely not liquid. If you're trying to sell during an economic downturn when people are more worried about their jobs than vacation, you may literally have no buyers—no matter how attractively you price the place.

Often, you can rent out a vacation home during the off-season to help defray some of your costs. While this income isn't likely to cover all of your expenses, it may help you carry a house that you couldn't otherwise afford.

If you plan on renting the house, consider the following:

- You may be able to deduct your financing fees on your tax return as a cost of doing business. This includes your closing costs, attorney's fees, and bank charges.

- Check out the property's rental history. How much did the previous owners charge? Did the same tenants rent year after year? That way you'll know what kind of cash stream to expect.

- Look for that extra "something." A ski chalet with a view of the slopes will bring more renters—and more money—than one that doesn't. So will a house on the lake or a beachfront condo with a health club and a pool.

ALL ABOUT CONDOS

Condominiums offer shared ownership. It's as though you bought a rental apartment and share in common, with all the other owners, everything *outside*: the grounds, the lobby and elevator, and the pool. Monthly maintenance fees are paid by each owner to keep the common areas in good order.

There are three types of condominiums: the "condo," the co-op, and the townhouse. A *condo* is what most people mean when they use the term "condominium." You own a particular unit, or apartment, in a building. Similarly, in a cooperatively-owned apartment (a *co-op*), you have the exclusive right to use a particular apartment. But unlike a condo, you don't actually own that apartment. Rather, you own a share in the company, which owns the entire property. *Townhouses*, meanwhile, are apartments arranged next to each other, not on top of each other like co-ops and condos. You share common walls, but you own the ground beneath your unit. One drawback: There are restrictions on what color you may paint the outside of your unit and how you may arrange flowers in a garden.

A condominum is often a wonderful first house. It costs less than a free-standing home, requires less upkeep, and, if you live in the place for a few years, builds up equity. You can then use that money for a down payment on a house.

Boom or Bust   During periods of strong economic growth, condos are often the last real estate properties to see price appreciation. In a down market, however, they're often the first to see price drops.

Maintenance charges—an important part of the condo's financial equation—are not frozen. Generally, it's true that the lower the maintenance fee, the higher the purchase price. (Similarly, houses with low taxes almost always cost more.) But maintenance charges can go up—quickly, in fact—if the owners of the whole building refinance their underlying mortgage and take out some of their original investment dollars.

Financing can be troublesome with condominiums, too. You can't always get a home equity loan on these properties. And some co-ops don't allow any financing. You must pay *cash*.

Seller Beware   Co-op boards are mighty picky. If you want to rent or sell the apartment that you "use" exclusively, all potential tenants must be checked for financial responsibility by the board first. If the board objects, you lose the sale.

In this lesson, you learned how to buy a vacation home and a condo. In the next lesson, you will learn how to borrow money against your house.

7

BORROWING AGAINST YOUR HOUSE

In this lesson, you'll learn how to borrow money against your home, using a home equity loan or a home equity line of credit.

TAPPING INTO YOUR HOME'S VALUE

Once you've invested your hard-earned dollars in a house, you can then turn around and borrow against that very same money to invest in something else. Tapping into your home's *equity*, in fact, has become increasingly popular these days because it offers you enormous borrowing power—at rates substantially lower than most consumer loans. Plus, unlike other consumer loans, these loans are tax deductible up to $100,000.

The good news is that this money is literally at your fingertips. You can use it to finance almost anything, including a college education, a trip to France, or that mail-order business you've always dreamed about. However, you're basically hocking the house. If you don't make the loan payments, the bank will grab your home.

HOW HOME EQUITY LOANS WORK

You should understand how a home equity loan works before you decide to take one. The "equity" in your home is the difference between what your home is currently worth, and how much money you still owe on your mortgage. For example, if your home is currently worth $200,000 and you still owe $75,000 on your mortgage, you have $125,000 in equity. (See Table 7.1.) Keep in mind that the equity in your home increases as the value (or price) of your home appreciates. That means, if you bought your home 10 years ago for $150,000 but it is presently worth $200,000, your equity has risen by $50,000.

TABLE 7.1 CALCULATING YOUR HOME'S EQUITY

Your Home's Current Value	$200,000
Less What You Owe on the Mortgage	–$75,000
Your Equity	$125,000

Home equity loans (also known as second mortgages) and home equity lines of credit allow you to borrow money against the equity in your house. Generally, banks, credit unions, and finance companies will lend you up to 80% of your equity. Using the example in Table 7.1, that means you could borrow up to 80% of $125,000—in this case, $100,000.

Competition and the low default record of home-equity loans has encouraged many lenders to allow borrowers to tap 100% of their home's equity.

A *home equity loan* works much like a first mortgage. You borrow a fixed amount of money, which you receive in a lump sum at the closing. You repay the loan in monthly installments over a fixed period, generally 10 or 15 years. The interest rate can be fixed, or variable (meaning the interest rate can rise or fall along with the movement of current interest rates).

A *home equity line of credit* (HELOC), meanwhile, works much like a revolving credit line typical of most major credit cards. At the outset of the loan, you're approved for a certain amount of money. That's your maximum credit line.

During the life of the loan, generally 15 years, you can draw on that credit line, in full or in part, whenever you want. All you do is write a check against the account or, in some cases, use a credit card. Because this is a *revolving* line of credit, you can borrow, pay back, borrow, pay back, and on and on, as often as you need.

Payback is generally very flexible, too. Your monthly payments are normally a percentage (about 2%) of the outstanding *balance* of the line—not of your maximum credit line. (See Table 7.2.)

TABLE 7.2   TYPICAL MONTHLY PAYMENT OF A HELOC WHEN YOU BORROW $10,000 AT 10% INTEREST

Principal	$10,000
Interest Paid	$1,000
Total P & I	$11,000
Monthly Payment	$220

Most HELOCs have both an *advance* term and a *repayment* term. During the advance term, you typically have unlimited access to your money, and you're often required to make interest-only payments. (Of course, you can replenish the amount you have borrowed, up to your maximum credit line, at any time.)

After the advance term has expired, you can't borrow any more money. You must now repay the balance over a specified time (known as the repayment term). Often, advance and repayment terms are 5-year advance, 10-year repayment; 10-year advance, 15-year repayment; or 10-year advance, 20-year repayment.

Nixed in Texas   By law, home equity loans are not permitted in the Lone Star State. But Texans can place a lien against their homes to pay taxes or to fund home improvements. (A lien means that you're using your house as collateral for the loan. Should you default on the payments, the bank gets the house.)

Home equity loans and home equity lines of credit both may offer a balloon feature. That means, you pay only interest on the loan each month, until the loan comes due. Then, the entire amount you borrowed is due, in one single payment! If you can't make that balloon payment—or you can't refinance the loan—you could lose the house.

Don't Let a Balloon Burst   Balloon loans can be tempting because they keep your monthly payments lower. But before you agree to this type of loan, ask the lender to agree *in writing* to refinance the final balance at term's end, if necessary.

WHICH COSTS MORE—A LOAN OR A LINE?

It would be simple if you could just compare their annual percentage rates (APR), but you can't. They're calculated differently.

Generally, with a home equity loan, all the financing fees are included in the annual percentage rate. However, the home-equity line's APR generally does *not* include all those fees, especially the points.

To comparison-shop, you'll have to compare the interest rates and itemize the additional fees yourself. In general, you can expect to pay fees similar to those paid when you got your first mortgage. Closing costs, which usually include a title search, survey, legal work (your attorney and the bank's attorney), and record charges, range from $500 and up.

New York Extra!   If you live in the Big Apple, your closing costs will also include *mortgage tax*—up to 2% of the amount you're borrowing. Fortunately, New York is the only state that levies this extra tax.

In addition, most lenders require some sort of appraisal of the property to determine just how much your home is worth. While some lenders will accept a "drive-by" appraisal, which is low-cost, others may insist on a full appraisal, which will cost you about $300.

Annual Fee   Like credit cards, some home-equity lines charge an annual fee, ranging from $30 to $75. The first year is usually free.

You generally must pay points on a home equity loan, but not on an equity line. (A point is equal to one percent of the loan amount.) However, some lenders will let you pay points on an equity line to get a lower interest rate.

For New Jerseyites Only   You're never charged points on a home equity loan in the Garden State.

Home equity lines are hot these days, so you'll probably find lenders offering more deals on lines than home equity loans. The competition is so great, in fact, that many lenders are offering lines with "zero closing costs." That means, the lender will waive all processing and closing fees, or cover the cost of them for you. The catch? You'll probably have to take an interest rate that's a half percentage point higher.

 Another Point About Points   Don't open a larger credit line than you need. If you're charged points, it's generally for the *maximum* line that you qualify for—whether you use all that money or not. The difference could be $1,000 or more.

THE RIGHT LOAN FOR YOU

A home equity *loan* is a good choice if:

- You need the money all at once. Perhaps you're adding a second-floor onto your home or starting a business.

- A revolving line of credit is too tempting. You'll keep dipping in for one purchase after another.

- You're on a limited budget. Because your monthly payments are fixed, you don't have to worry when interest rates rise.

- You won't need to borrow more money next year or the year after that. Every time you rewrite a second mortgage for a larger amount, you'll pay mortgage costs all over again.

A home equity *line* of credit is a good choice if:

- You need flexibility. Over the next four years, you have to pay your son's tuition every year. Plus, you'd like to put a new roof on the house and remodel the kitchen.

- You're a disciplined spender. You won't touch that money for frivolous expenditures. Otherwise, it's easy to get into deep debt—and stay there—since payments can be stretched out over several years.

- You need an emergency cash fund for unforeseen expenses.

 Job Insecurity If you think that you might be laid off in the near future, now's the time to apply for that HELOC—while you still qualify. This emergency fund could bridge the gap until you find another job.

In this lesson, you learned how to borrow money against your house with a home equity loan or a home equity line of credit. In the next lesson, you will learn how to use a home equity line of credit.

8

THE MULTI-PURPOSE HOME EQUITY LINE

In this lesson, you'll learn how to use a home equity line of credit.

WHEN TO USE A HOME EQUITY LINE

Home equity lines are not just for home improvements. You can borrow against your house to do just about anything: buy a car, send your children to college, invest in a franchise, or even consolidate your high-interest-rate credit card debt. Of course, you can still remodel the kitchen, too.

Initially, you're more likely to feel comfortable tapping into your home's equity to buy another house or to fix the current one. Buying a car or some stock with the money may seem too risky.

However, using a line of credit to invest can be a sound idea if you analyze the investment and your current financial situation carefully. Don't borrow so much money, for instance, that you stand to lose your house should your investment suddenly go sour. An equity line is attractive to many borrowers because:

- It's easy to apply for. Some lenders now take applications over the phone and approve loans within 24 hours.

- It's affordable. Rates are currently running 1 to 3 points above "prime." (Prime is the interest rate that banks charge to their largest customers—namely, mega-corporations—when these customers want to borrow money. Individuals, however, never actually borrow money at the prime rate. Instead, this rate acts as a benchmark. Individuals pay prime—plus a bit more.)

- It's the only borrowing source that many people have.

- It's tax deductible—unlike other consumer loans.

THE RULES FOR USING LINES OF CREDIT

Home equity lines of credit (HELOCs) generally offer a *variable* interest rate that is adjusted monthly and that rises and falls along with the general movement of interest rates. Some equity lines now offer an interest rate *cap*, too. Your rate can go only so high or so low. A common cap, for example, might be that your interest rate can rise no higher than 5 or 6 points more than the rate you started with.

To lure customers, some lenders are currently offering "teaser" rates that are substantially lower than the going rate. Unfortunately, these low rates usually last for just six months—or less. And you often have to borrow a minimum amount, which, in some cases, can be as much as $20,000.

Convertible Option   If variable rates make you nervous, you can get a fixed rate on the balance of your credit line. The drawback is that your credit line is frozen from that point on. You can't borrow and repay and then borrow some more.

Planning on making just the minimum payment each month? That's fine—if you're temporarily strapped for cash. But consistently paying the minimum amount will make this a mighty expensive loan. Because most home equity lines don't have any prepayment penalties, you can pay back the loan whenever you want. Depending on what you use the money for, here's a reasonable repayment schedule to follow:

Auto Loan: 4 years

Debt Consolidation: 18 months

Home Improvement: 7 years

It's important that you understand how the home equity line of credit compares to traditional sources of borrowing.

A HOME EQUITY LINE OF CREDIT VS. CREDIT CARD DEBT

Many people use an equity line to consolidate their various credit card debts. Basically, you're exchanging several smaller bills for one larger bill. In theory, you should save money because credit cards charge substantially higher interest rates than do home equity lines of credit. (See Table 8.1.)

TABLE 8.1   COMPARING INTEREST RATES*
Average Interest Rates

	HOME EQUITY LINE OF CREDIT	CREDIT CARD	AUTO LOANS
New York	7.30	18.85	9.22
Chicago	9.28	15.90	8.54
Los Angeles	9.92	18.95	10.09
Philadelphia	7.57	15.90	8.67
Detroit	10.32	16.48	9.99

Source: Bank Rate Monitor, North Palm Beach, FL

For example, assume you owe $4,000 on your credit cards, at 18% interest. If you take out a home equity loan at 10% to pay off that credit card debt, you'll cut your annual interest charges nearly in half—from $720 to $400. You can use that $320 to repay the loan faster, which will then enable you to invest your money more profitably elsewhere.

Generally, that's a smart move to make. Remember, too, the interest paid on home equity loans is tax-deductible, up to $100,000, and the interest paid on credit card debt isn't.

But a lower-interest rate doesn't always mean more money in your pocket. In fact, a home equity line could wind up costing you more than that old credit card debt if:

- You keep on borrowing. Assume you've consolidated your credit card debt using an equity line. However, six months later you've charged your cards to the max again. Now you have two monstrous debts to pay off—and the bank could foreclose on your house if you don't make your payments.

- You treat that credit line as permanent debt, to be paid off when you sell the house. In the long run, your interest payments can be as hefty as those you would've paid on the original credit card debt. Home equity debt, like credit card debt, can stretch on for ten years or more if you simply make the minimum payment each month. Remember that the longer you're paying interest, the more it's going to cost you.

A HOME EQUITY LINE OF CREDIT VS. OTHER CONSUMER DEBT

Using your home equity line to invest in a new car, antique dining room furniture, or a state-of-the-art computer system is often a good idea because you can deduct the interest on your taxes. (The interest on car loans and personal loans is *not* tax-deductible.) Home equity interest rates are also generally lower than the rates of most other consumer loans.

When Rates Rise   Consumer loans offer a fixed rate; home equity lines usually don't. Should interest rates rise, you may have more protection (and a lot more piece of mind) with a traditional consumer loan.

It makes sense to tap your home's equity if you already have an equity line open. It'll cost you nothing to get access to the money, and you can get it immediately. If you don't have an equity line, however, you'll probably have to pay some fees up front to open one—which can be substantial, as we learned in the last lesson—and that might offset the money you'd save in taxes.

If you're buying a car, be sure to check your financing options with the auto dealer. In some cases, dealers offer low-cost promotional loans that are cheaper than a home equity line. (See Figure 8.1.) Unfortunately, you can't simply compare the annual percentage rates of interest (APRs) of the two loans because they're figured differently. Generally, the auto loan's APR includes all additional fees, while the home equity line of credit does not.

Perpetual Car Debt   If you finance your car with a home equity line—and take more than five years to repay the loan—it's possible that you could still be paying off the car when it's time to get rid of it. Then, you'll borrow more money to buy a replacement, and you'll be even deeper in debt.

USING A HOME EQUITY LINE OF CREDIT TO MAKE AN INVESTMENT

Want to buy some hot stocks, but the only money available is the equity in your house? There's nothing wrong with taking the money out of your house and investing it elsewhere *if* you've properly investigated the investment and you can afford to take a loss.

Don't Risk Everything!   Don't—repeat, don't— drain the last drop of equity in your house if you'll lose everything should your investment fail. No matter what anyone promises, no investment is 100% guaranteed.

Borrowing to fund an investment makes good financial sense when you expect that investment to yield more than it's costing you to borrow from your home equity line. If you're investing in stocks or bonds you may not see that higher expected return right away, but you should over the long term. For example, if you're paying 9.5% interest on the money you've borrowed, the bonds that you've invested in should earn more than that over time.

Is It Worth It?   When you're weighing interest payments and expected investment returns, don't forget an often-overlooked factor in the equation: you must pay taxes on all profits from your investment.

In Case of Emergency   If you use your home equity line to fund a stock purchase and then find yourself struggling to make the monthly payments, you could always sell the stocks to pay back some of the loan.

In this lesson, you learned how to use a home equity line of credit. In the next lesson, you will learn how to refinance your house.

REFINANCING YOUR HOUSE

In this lesson, you'll learn how to borrow money against your house, through refinancing.

THE IMPORTANCE OF INTEREST RATES

Interest rates move constantly. When you take out a mortgage, you lock into an interest rate, either for a short period of time (an adjustable-rate mortage), or a long period of time (a fixed-rate mortgage). Whenever interest rates drop, you can rewrite your mortgage using the more favorable rate. That's called refinancing. When you refinance, you take out a new, lower-rate mortgage to pay off your old, higher-rate mortgage. After refinancing, your monthly mortgage payments are generally less because you're paying a lower mortgage interest rate.

Most people refinance for one of two reasons: to take advantage of a low interest rate and thus lower their monthly mortgage payments, or to tap into their home's equity, called a "cash-out refi." With this type of refinancing, you trade in your current mortgage for a larger one and pocket the extra money. You can then use that surplus cash to invest in something else, like a country home.

If you're a disciplined saver, however, you don't need a cash-out refi. Simply refinance the same size mortgage at the lower interest rate and invest the difference yourself. Unfortunately, many people who use this method might find that they never see that monthly savings. The money just gets eaten up by daily expenses.

> **!** **Cash-out Catch** Most lenders won't let you borrow more than 75% or 80% of your home's current appraised value. That could be troublesome if you have a high mortgage already or the value of your home has declined. If you don't qualify, you could always take out a home equity line of credit (see lessons 7 and 8) instead.

You may not get the lowest advertised interest rate on your refinancing if your mortgage amount is more than $202,300. Loans above this amount—called "jumbo" loans—often have interest rates 1/2% higher than smaller loans.

PICKING THE RIGHT MORTGAGE

When you refinance, you don't necessarily have to stick with the same type of mortgage you picked when you bought your house. If interest rates are especially low, for instance, now might be a good time to switch from an adjustable-rate mortgage to a fixed-rate mortgage.

How long do you plan on holding the new mortgage? Knowing this will help you determine which kind of mortgage to pick. For example, if you want a new mortgage for a short period of time—five years or less—you'll probably want an adjustable-rate mortgage rather than a fixed-rate. With a very low first year's interest rate—and a pre-adjustment cap of 2%—it's almost guaranteed that you'll pay less than a 30-year fixed-rate for at least two years. By the time the fixed rate proves to be a better deal, you'll be ready to pay off your mortgage, or refinance again.

Obviously, the biggest savings will come from paying *less* interest. If you're comfortable with the monthly payments you're now making, it's possible that you could refinance into a mortgage with a shorter term—15 years instead of your current 30—for the very same monthly payment you now have.

While this won't put any extra cash into your pocket right now for investments, it will build equity in your home twice as fast, allowing you to borrow larger sums against it in the near future. It'll cost you a lot less in interest, too, for as long as you hold the loan.

THE COSTS INVOLVED

When you refinance, you also must go through "closing." Generally, that'll cost you between $500 and $5,000. As you may remember from when you got your first mortgage, you're charged for everything from a termite inspection to a credit check to an attorney's fee.

 Closing Costs   Closing costs are what it will cost you to get a mortgage. The higher the costs to secure a new mortgage, the longer it will take to realize the savings of that refinanced mortgage.

Stick with the Same Lender   Ask the original lender of your mortgage about refinancing options. Sometimes you can simply rewrite your present mortgage without going through a full-scale refinance.

The major cost in obtaining any mortgage is *points*. (One point equals one percent of the loan amount.) Since points are really a prepayment of interest, you'll typically get a lower interest rate if you pay more points.

Private Mortgage Insurance (PMI)   If you put less than 20% down on your house originally, your first mortgage probably required PMI. You can drop that coverage now—and save 1/4% on your new interest rate—if your new mortgage is 80% or less than the appraised value of the house.

WHEN TO REFINANCE

If you refinance to lower your monthly payments, you'll almost immediately pocket a few extra dollars every month. But when will it really pay off? In other words, how long will it take to recoup the extra cost of refinancing?

Here's a quick way to figure it out:

1. Add up all of your closing costs. Include any prepayment penalties.

2. Calculate the difference between your current

monthly mortgage payment and your projected monthly mortgage payment after the refinance.

3. Divide your total closing costs by the difference in monthly payments. The result is the number of months it will take to recoup the cost of refinancing. (See Table 9.1.) After that time, you'll save money every month.

TABLE 9.1   RECOUPING THE COST OF REFINANCING*

Current monthly mortgage payment	$1,500
New monthly mortgage payment	$1,200
Difference in monthly payments	$300
Total closing costs	$3,000
Divided by difference in payments	300
Time needed to recoup cost	10 months

*Source: HSH Associates, Butler, NJ

This is the traditional refinance rule: Don't refinance your mortgage unless you can reduce your interest rate by at least two percentage points. Many experts say that formula is too simplistic these days, however. For some people—especially those with mortgages of $500,000 or more—improving their interest rate by as little as one-half of 1% can be enough incentive to refinance.

Basically, it makes sense to refinance if:

- You're planning to live in your home well beyond the time it will take to recoup the costs of refinancing.

- Fixed rates are exceedingly low and you have an adjustable-rate mortgage that you would like to switch to a fixed-rate mortgage.

REFINANCING VS. A HOME EQUITY LINE OF CREDIT

If you're going to tap the equity in your house for investment funds, which is the better way to do it: refinance with a larger first mortgage or take out a home equity line of credit? You'll have to compare the costs of both options. (You'll have to plug in the actual numbers yourself to see which is the better deal.)

1. **Initial Costs.** Refinancing probably costs more to set up because you have to pay points and the other costs associated with closing. Most lenders don't charge points on home equity lines, however. Due to competition, many now offer "zero closing costs" deals, too.

2. **Interest Rate.** The rate on a refinanced first mortgage is generally lower than the interest rate on a home equity line. But what about keeping your first mortgage *and* taking out a fixed-rate second mortgage? You'll have to comparison-shop the rates.

3. **Flexibility.** With a home equity line you borrow what you need, when you need it. And you can control the size of your monthly repayments. When you refinance, you get one lump sum payment, which is paid back monthly over a fixed period of time.

In this lesson, you learned how to borrow money against your house, through refinancing. In the next lesson, you will learn how to borrow an unsecured loan, take out a cash advance, and use overdraft checking.

10

BORROWING AGAINST YOURSELF

In this lesson, you'll learn how to borrow an unsecured loan, take out a cash advance, and use overdraft checking.

When you borrow money from a bank or any other lender, you generally must put up some collateral—property such as a house, stocks and bonds, or your life insurance policy—that you use to guarantee, or *secure*, the loan. If you don't pay back the loan, the lender will seize your collateral as payment.

But what if you rent an apartment instead of owning your own home? Or, you recently graduated from college and don't own anything of value yet? What if your spouse left you, taking all your possessions, and hasn't been heard from in two years? Could you still borrow money? Yes. It'll just cost more.

BORROWING AN UNSECURED PERSONAL LOAN

An unsecured personal loan is when you borrow money from a lender, based solely upon your current salary and credit history. Often, you can borrow as much as $25,000 or as little as $1,500. However, if you don't repay the loan, the lender will sue.

To determine whether or not to offer you a loan (referred to as your "creditworthiness"), lenders will ask you to fill out a loan application. The following information will probably be included on the application:

1. **Your Credit History.** Lenders want to see that you've repaid your past debts—on time and in full. If you've filed for bankruptcy within the last seven years, for instance, you'll be turned down immediately.

2. **Your Debt-to-Income Ratio.** Each lender uses his own magic numbers to figure out how much debt you can afford, given your current income. In general, most lenders want your consumer debt to constitute no more than 40 or 50% of your gross income.

3. **The Kind of Debt You Have.** While too much debt might prevent you from getting that loan, so might too "little" debt. Lenders like to see that you're an experienced debtor, who has a variety of creditors. This is known as a "thick" file. Too few creditors—or none at all—means you have a "thin" file.

4. **Your Stability.** Most lenders like to see a minimum of two years of steady employment in the same job (or at least the same field), and at least two years of residency in the same community.

5. **Your Intentions.** Lenders will ask why you want the money. The most common uses include funding a vacation or wedding, paying off doctor bills, or consolidating debt.

Out of Business Lenders will not grant an unsecured loan to start up, or expand, a business.

The most common unsecured loans include money withdrawn from your line of credit on a credit card (called a cash advance) or your personal checking account (called overdraft checking).

Naturally, the interest rate is higher for unsecured loans than secured loans. The following table shows typical interest rates on unsecured loans. The repayment period is generally shorter, too—usually one to five years.

TABLE 10.1   THE COST OF AN UNSECURED LOAN*

	INTEREST RATE
Personal Loan	12.45%
Cash Advance	32.94%
Overdraft Checking	15.5%

Source: Bankcard Holders of America, McLean, VA

TAKING A CASH ADVANCE

A cash advance is a cash loan that is obtained through a credit card such as Visa or MasterCard. Most credit card issuers allow cash advances. The only exceptions are gas and retail cards, like Mobil and J.C. Penney.

You can get a cash advance at most banks or automated teller machines (ATMs). Generally, you can borrow up to your credit limit. But since most ATMs won't let you withdraw more than $300 per day, you'll have to do a "live" transaction at the bank if you need a larger sum all at once.

Cash advances are probably the simplest way to borrow money—but they're also the most *expensive*. Interest rates are often higher for cash advances than for purchases. And many issuers charge an additional "cash advance fee," ranging from $2 to $20, every time you take an advance.

Compounded Differently   Even if your lender offers you the same interest rate for cash advances as it does for credit card purchases, you may still be charged more. The interest for purchases is often compounded monthly while the interest for cash advances may be compounded daily. (A credit card issuer *compounds* your debt payment by adding interest on top of the interest that you already owe for the loan. The more frequently the issuer compounds the interest on your debt, the more money you owe.)

Worst of all, there is no grace period. Interest starts accruing immediately, the very moment you withdraw your first dollar. Unfortunately, there is no way to avoid paying interest, even if you pay all the money back by the end of the month.

Some issuers do offer interest-free grace periods on cash advances. That doesn't necessarily mean you're getting a good deal, though, since they usually charge cash advance fees instead. Sometimes the cash advance fee is more expensive than simply paying one month's interest on the advance.

Let's look at an example: On April 5th, you take out a cash advance of $300 (the average advance). You pay the money back on the 30th. You're charged one month's interest at 18.5%—plus an advance fee of $2.50. Your real interest rate (for just one month), which includes the advance fee, is 32.94%.

Rate Not Fixed Forever   Cash advances are not like other bank loans. A fixed rate does not always mean a *fixed* rate. The credit card issuer—in most cases, a bank—can raise its credit card interest rate at any time. All the bank has to do is give you 15 days advance notice, in writing. Then it can apply the new, higher rate to your outstanding balance, as well as to all new charges.

Not in Delaware   Credit card issuers can't just raise their rates in the state of Delaware. Under Delaware law, consumers have 30 days to decline acceptance of the new terms. If they stop using their credit card, they can then make monthly payments toward their existing balance at the old rate.

USING OVERDRAFT CHECKING

Another common feature of many checking accounts is actually a type of loan. Overdraft checking lets you borrow more money than you have in your checking account—often up to $25,000. Like cash advances, you can make these withdrawals at the bank or an ATM.

Banks will generally grant you "overdraft" privileges once you've established a checking account at their institution and they've checked out your credit history. (This procedure is not as extensive or time-consuming as it is for other loans.)

Most banks charge transaction fees every time you withdraw the cash, although there's usually no fee to set up the credit line initially. There also may be restrictions on the amount of money that you can withdraw. For instance, you generally can't take out an odd number like $57. It has to be rounded to the nearest 10 or be some multiple of 50.

Like cash advances, overdraft checking is expensive. The interest rate is considerably higher—sometimes as much as 3 percentage points higher—than what you'd pay for a more traditional unsecured loan. The main advantage: You can get your hands on needed funds instantly.

If you only need the borrowed funds for a few months, however, try this smart borrowing alternative: Ask your banker for a *really* short-term loan, like three or six months. The interest rate is likely to be less than that charged for overdraft checking. You may even be able to renew the loan once or twice. Of course, this approach works best if you're on friendly terms with your banker and you keep several accounts there.

Use Only in Case of Emergency   The trouble with overdraft checking is that it's so easy to continue withdrawing more and more money. And, except for a small monthly payment, the bank isn't likely to pressure you to repay the full debt any time soon. So it could cost you a lot, especially if you stretch the payments out over several months or years.

In this lesson, you learned how to borrow an unsecured loan, take out a cash advance, and use overdraft checking. In the next lesson, you will learn how to borrow money on margin.

11

Borrowing Against Stocks, Bonds, and Mutual Funds

In this lesson, you'll learn how to borrow money on margin.

Borrowing Against Your Investments

Most of you invest money in stocks, bonds, and mutual funds for the *long* haul. That means, you don't touch those funds until you're ready to retire or it's time to send your children to college. Luckily, Wall Street is an eager money lender. You can invest your money in stocks and bonds—and then borrow against that investment to make purchases or another investment. This is a margin loan.

Margin Loan A margin loan is a loan that a broker makes to a customer, which is secured by the stocks and bonds that the customer owns. Usually, a margin loan is used to buy more securities, but you can borrow for other purposes, too, such as consolidating higher-cost debt, buying a car, financing the down payment on a house, or expanding your business.

Margin loans can be a good borrowing option because rates are often lower than those offered by other lenders. Typically, interest rates run 0.75% to 2.75% above the firm's base rate, which fluctuates according to current interest rates.

Also, getting a margin loan is quick and easy. Unlike most mortgages and home equity loans, margin loans have no closing costs, no pre-set repayment schedule, and no lengthy applications to complete.

 No Repayments The entire margin loan, plus interest, is payable when the securities are sold. Of course, you could always save on interest costs by making monthly payments.

BORROWING ON MARGIN

Just as a mortgage loan enables you to buy a more expensive home than you could otherwise afford, a margin loan lets you buy more shares of an investment than you would otherwise be able to purchase. And, the more securities you buy, the greater the potential for gain.

Let's assume you have $3,000 to invest and you want to buy a $20 stock. You can buy 150 shares outright. Or, you can buy an additional 150 shares on margin, for a total of 300 shares. With a margin loan, you can basically buy twice as many shares of stock—for the same amount of money. (See Table 11.1.)

TABLE 11.1   COMMON STOCK OF CUTTING EDGE CORPORATION
Current Price = $20 per share

CASH CLIENT		MARGIN CLIENT	
Buys:	150 shares	Buys:	300 shares
Cost:	$3,000	Cost:	$6,000
Owes:	$0	Owes:	$3,000

Should the stock price go up, the margin client will reap substantially more profits than the cash investor. Using the example in Table 11.1, the shares go up by 25%, to $25. The cash investor would make $750; the margin investor, $1,500—minus interest costs. (See Table 11.2.)

TABLE 11.2

CASH CLIENT	MARGIN CLIENT
Sells 150 shares: $3,750	Sells 300 shares: $7,500
Less cost of shares: $3,000	*Less* cost of shares: $3,000
	Less margin loan: $3,000
Profit: $750	Profit: $1,500*
* Does not include interest charged on the margin loan.	

Of course, these numbers reflect a stock price that goes *up*. If the stock price goes down—as it's apt to do at some point or another—margin loans don't look nearly as attractive. In fact, they look downright awful.

 Double-Edged Sword   A margin loan lets you reap twice the amount of profits if your stocks rise. But it also allows you to lose twice as much—plus interest—should your shares drop in price.

Let's look at the example again. You bought those same 150 shares in the Cutting Edge Corporation. Only this time the stock has fallen by 25%, to $15 per share. The cash investor would lose $750. And the margin investor? More than double that amount—$1,500 plus interest.

TABLE 11.3

CASH CLIENT	MARGIN CLIENT
Sells 150 shares for: $2,250	Sells 300 shares for: $4,500
Less cost of shares: $3,000	*Less* cost: $3,000
	Less margin loan: $3,000
Loss: $750	Loss: $1,500*
*Does not include interest charged on the margin loan.	

Margin loans can also be troublesome because of a small but important detail called a *margin call*. If the market suddenly drops—and your stock takes a nosedive—you'll have to repay part of the loan, immediately. Your broker will expect you to deposit more cash or securities into your account, usually within four days. If you're short of funds, the broker will simply sell some of the shares in your account—no questions asked. Then, you can be sold out of your stock immediately. And that could mean a serious financial loss for you.

You should also understand how margin loans work. There are no pre-set borrowing limits. The amount of money that you may borrow depends largely upon how much equity you have in your margin account, and the limits set by your particular brokerage firm. For instance: You can generally borrow up to 50% of the value of certain stocks, mutual funds, and corporate bonds, and up to 85% for municipal bonds.

 U.S. Government Approved   You can borrow even more—up to 95%—when you borrow against Treasury securites, because they're backed by the U.S. government.

 Mutual Fund Margining   Some mutual funds can be margined, too—usually up to 50%. But since the average investor puts money in a mutual fund to build a retirement nest egg, most people don't feel comfortable putting those funds at risk.

ARRANGING A MARGIN LOAN

Talk to your broker. Generally, you have to open a margin account. While the equity in that account will naturally fluctutate with the market value of your securities, you must maintain a minimum level of equity at all times—usually $2,000, even if you're borrowing less than that amount. That means, you must keep $2,000 in cash in the account, or twice that amount in securities.

 Stock Preference   Most investors use securities that they already own, rather than cash, as collateral when opening up a margin account.

Generally, you can get a margin loan simply by using your credit card or writing a check against your margin account.

 Not Eligible   You can't take a margin loan on Certificates of Deposit (CDs), unlisted common stocks, over-the-counter stocks that are not federally approved, series EE Savings Bonds, and mutual funds (for the first 30 days).

If your stocks keep going up, you can borrow on a margin loan forever. Or, interest charges and a sudden drop in the market may force you to sell all of your shares tomorrow.

Some people do invest on margin for long periods of time. But, generally speaking, you need either a fast rise or a substantial rise in the stock price. Otherwise, mediocre profits will be quickly wiped out by the interest charges compounding in your account month after month.

When to Borrow on Margin

A margin loan is a *good* idea if:

- You have the temperment to take risks. A slight dip in the market won't make you a nervous wreck.

- You have the extra cash or securities on-hand to meet a margin call.

- You're a seasoned investor. You want to leverage your investments to build up your nest egg faster.

- You've inherited stocks—and you need some cash. But, because of fluctuations in the market, it would not be a good time to sell those shares.

A margin loan is a *bad* idea if:

- You think that stock prices only go up, up, up.

- Funds are tight. If you received a margin call, you'd have to sell the shares in your account.

- You're borrowing against your retirement fund, or your only source of savings.

In this lesson, you learned how to borrow money on margin. In the next lesson, you will learn how to borrow money from your retirement funds.

12

BORROWING AGAINST YOUR RETIREMENT FUND

In this lesson, you'll learn how to borrow money from various retirement funds.

USING RETIREMENT FUNDS

Although these funds are meant first and foremost for retirement, you can often take a loan against the assets—without depleting your retirement nest egg. More and more companies currently allow employees to borrow from these plans; some still don't, mainly because of the paperwork involved. To find out what's permissible, check out the "loan provision" in your particular plan.

BORROWING MONEY FROM AN INDIVIDUAL RETIREMENT ACCOUNT (IRA)

Under an Individual Retirement Account (IRA), an individual employee who is not covered by a pension or profit-sharing plan at his job can put up to 15% of his earnings (up to a maximum of $2,000) in this retirement plan every year. If you earn less than $2,000, of course, the whole amount can be contributed. And you can stash away an additional $250 per year for an unemployed spouse. Your money will grow and compound tax-free until it is withdrawn. While you can easily take a loan from an IRA, consider carefully the penalties and tax implications of these loans.

Normally, you must pay a 10% penalty on any withdrawals from an IRA before age 59 1/2. But you can "borrow" money from your IRA, penalty- and tax-free. The catch? You must return the funds within 60 days. And you can borrow such funds only once per year.

This is ready money and it could buy you time in an emergency. But it's very easy to get into trouble with this kind of debt. Many borrowers still find themselves strapped for cash when the loan comes due 60 days later. If you can't pay it back at that time, your loan will be treated like a withdrawal. You'll have to pay that 10% early-withdrawal penalty, plus income tax (determined by your age and tax bracket).

To borrow money from an IRA, write to your IRA custodian and request the amount you need, noting that you plan to put the money back within 60 days.

BORROWING MONEY FROM A KEOGH PLAN

A Keogh plan is a popular retirement plan for self-employed people. It comes in four varieties. A "profit-sharing" Keogh allows a self-employed individual to earmark as much as 13.04% of his net earnings (up to $30,000) per year for retirement. A "money-purchase" Keogh allows you to contribute as much as 20% of your earnings (up to $30,000) per year. A "combination" Keogh combines both of the above plans' options, so you have greater flexibility and the highest contribution limit. And a "defined-benefit" Keogh lets you make even larger deposits, depending upon your age and your income. In all four plans, contributions grow tax-deferred.

There is an important distinction between the two most common Keoghs. With a *profit-sharing Keogh*, you don't have to put money in every year, and you can vary the amount that you put away from one year to the next. With a *money-purchase Keogh*, however, you can put away a larger percentage of your money, but you must contribute a fixed percentage of your income every year.

Borrowing from a Keogh Plan is complicated. Generally, if you're self-employed and the only participant in the plan, you can't borrow any money. However, if your business is incorporated, then you probably can. If you're an employee—that means you have no financial stake in the business—you can probably borrow from your Keogh, too.

If you meet these qualifications, you can usually borrow up to $50,000 from your Keogh, payable over five years. Some plans require your spouse's agreement—in writing and notarized—to take out the loan.

BORROWING MONEY FROM A 401(K), 403(B), OR PROFIT-SHARING PLAN

A *401(k)* is a savings plan that lets you, the employee, set aside part of your salary each year for retirement. You don't pay income taxes now on the funds deposited (but you must pay Social Security taxes). You don't pay any taxes on the earnings either, until you withdraw them when you retire. Many companies encourage employees to contribute to these savings plans by matching contributions. Generally, you can contribute from 5 to 15% of your salary, depending upon your plan's limitations.

A *403(b)* plan works similarly. 403(b) plans are designed for teachers, workers at non-profit hospitals, and employees of religious and charitable organizations. A third retirement plan is called a *profit-sharing plan*. Under this plan, an employee's share of the company's yearly profits are put into a retirement savings plan, tax-free, until he or she retires.

It's often possible to borrow from any of these three retirement plans. Generally, you can get a loan just by making a quick phone call to your company's human resources or benefits department. There is no credit check, since the funds in your account serve as collateral. Few companies bother to even ask why you want the money anymore. Some plans do charge a small loan-initiation fee and an annual processing fee, but, compared to getting a similar loan at a bank, these costs are generally minimal.

By law, you can borrow no more than 50% of your account's assets, up to $50,000. Repayments begin immediately—usually quarterly, via automatic payroll deduction—and typically must be completed within five years. However, if you're borrowing money to buy a house (it must be your primary residence), you frequently can take as long as 20 to 30 years to repay the money.

The interest rate for such a loan is usually attractive, too—prime, plus one or two percentage points. But the best part is that since you're essentially borrowing your own money, you pay the interest back to yourself. That means a loan won't really stop your nest egg from growing.

Here's how it works. Suppose your 401(k) returned an average
of 12.5%. If you borrowed some of that money—at an interest
rate of 10%, let's say, and you paid it back over five years—
your retirement account still would have grown. But the rate
of return would have been slightly lower (2.5% less) and the
asset accumulation less, too. (Why? The money was returned
to the fund over a five-year period rather than earning interest
from day one.)

If you get laid off or change jobs while you have a loan outstanding against your retirement fund, you'll probably have to
repay the money immediately. A few companies will let you
continue the payments as scheduled, but more likely you'll
have to repay the loan upon termination or in 30 or 60 days,
depending upon the plan. What happens if you can't repay so
quickly? The loan is then considered a withdrawal and you'll
owe federal taxes on the loan amount—plus that 10% early-
withdrawal penalty if you're younger than 59 1/2.

Last Resort   Often, you can withdraw money
from your 401(k) plan to pay for college tuition or
to buy a home *if* you have no other resources
available. It's called a "hardship withdrawal."
You're not actually *borrowing* the money, though:
You're taking it out—for good. If your company's
plan allows withdrawals (and not all of them do),
you'll pay federal taxes on the amount you take
out, plus that old 10% early-withdrawal penalty if
you're younger than 59 1/2. This is not a smart
borrowing option, but it can be a lifesaver if you
really need the cash.

You should borrow from your retirement plan if:

- The cost of borrowing money from your plan is less than borrowing from another source, such as a bank, a credit union, or an auto dealer.

- Your job is secure.

- You're planning to use the loan to invest in something substantial—a house, a car, or tuition—rather than a luxury item, like a vacation in Paris.

- You plan on doing it just once or twice. One five-year loan will have little impact ultimately on your long-term retirement savings, but dipping in continually might reduce your savings substantially.

- The interest rate you pay on your loan is higher than the return your retirement plan was earning on its investments. Example: Your bond fund was earning 7% annually. Now you're paying 10.5% to borrow that money. As a result, you're plunking an additional 3.5% into your retirement nest egg.

In this lesson, you have learned how to borrow money from retirement funds. In the next lesson, you'll learn how to borrow against life insurance policies and certificates of deposit.

13

Borrowing Against Insurance Policies and Certificates of Deposit

In this lesson, you'll learn how to borrow against your life insurance policy and your certificates of deposit.

Borrowing Against Your Insurance Policy

Sometimes it's simply smarter to borrow from your own funds, instead of going to banks and private lenders. In the two previous lessons, you've learned that you can tap into your retirement nest egg, as well as your stocks and bonds. But did you know that you can borrow money from your insurance policy, too?

In fact, this may be the smartest loan of all. But you won't know that until you've done some calculating, because the real cost of borrowing is higher than the stated interest rate.

You can generally borrow from most "permanent" insurance policies, such as whole, ordinary, universal, adjustable, and variable life, because they have a *cash value*. "Term" insurance, however, has no cash value so you can't borrow from it.

 Cash Value   Cash value is the amount of money you'd receive if you cashed in your policy today— before its maturity or your death. This is less than the *face value*, which is the amount of money (written on the face of the policy) that's paid at death or at policy maturity.

When you tap into your life insurance policy, you're basically borrowing *against* the policy's "cash value," using it as collateral. Your cash value will continue to earn interest—even when you borrow against it. But, in many cases, it will earn interest at a lower rate than it did before. That's the hidden cost.

Let's assume that your whole-life policy now earns 8.5% interest. If you borrow money from the policy, that interest rate may be cut to 6.5% (or less) on the portion of the cash value that you've borrowed. (Most policies guarantee a minimum interest rate of 4 or 5%.) So far, this loan is costing you 2% in lost interest.

Of course, you have to pay interest on the borrowed money, too. In most cases, the stated interest rate currently hovers somewhere around 8% (about what you'd earn on a Treasury Bond), which is less than a typical personal loan and much, much cheaper than borrowing on a credit card.

The true cost of the loan, however, is 10%. Here's how to calculate it: 2% in lost earnings (also known as the opportunity cost) plus the 8% interest rate. (See Table 13.1.)

TABLE 13.1   **WHAT AN INSURANCE POLICY LOAN REALLY COSTS**

Interest earned on policy's cash value	8.5%
Less interest earned on cash value you've borrowed against	–6.5%
Opportunity cost	2.0%
Plus stated interest rate to borrow funds	8.0%
True cost of borrowing	10.0%

MORE FACTS ABOUT A LIFE INSURANCE LOAN

The good news is that this loan need never be repaid out of pocket. (If you want to, you can repay it whenever you like.) The interest is generally compounded and subtracted from your policy's remaining cash value, which will simply decrease by the amount of the loan. For example: You have a $500,000 policy and you borrow $100,000. That'll leave a $400,000 death benefit remaining.

 Keep In Mind   Most people buy life insurance as financial protection for survivors. If you borrow against your policy—and don't pay it back—there may not be enough money left to support them. That could put your family's financial well-being in jeopardy.

Your death benefit will rise again, as you repay the loan. But, in later years, you may have to pay more in premiums to make up for that lower cash-value growth when the loan was outstanding.

This is especially true if you have a level death benefit featured in some insurance policies, in which you pay just enough insurance to make up the difference between your cash value and the death benefit.

You can often borrow up to 90% of your cash value. If you just bought the policy a few years ago, however, that could mean next to nothing. Commissions and start-up costs eat up most of your early premiums, so there's very little cash value until year four or so.

Most people borrow against a life insurance policy to meet short-term needs, such as buying a car, financing a wedding, or starting up a business, because it's so easy to borrow money this way. Virtually no questions are asked. Just call your insurance agent. There are no applications or credit checks, and in many cases, you'll receive a check within 7 to 10 days.

> **!** **Address Change**   To prevent scams, some insurance companies will automatically mail the check to the address listed in your file—no matter what you say on the phone. So if you've moved recently, you'd better update your insurance file before arranging for a loan.

Borrowing Against a Certificate of Deposit (CD)

A certificate of deposit (CD) is savings deposited in a bank or savings and loan institution, which earns a guaranteed interest rate, for a specified period of time. For example: A consumer deposits $1,000 at a bank and in return receives a *certificate*, guaranteeing 7% interest for five years. Normally, the longer the term, the higher the interest rate.

CDs are ideal, therefore, for money that must be kept safe—like the nest egg you need for a house down payment or a new car next year. While they generally offer higher interest rates than their passbook savings cousins, you can't tap into a CD without incurring an early withdrawal penalty.

If you have some funds tied up in a CD—and you need money right now to invest elsewhere—most lenders will let you borrow money against the account. Like an insurance policy loan, you're not taking your own money out directly. Instead, you're borrowing money against your account and using the certificate of deposit as collateral.

This may, or may not, be a smart idea. A personal loan will generally cost you 10.5% these days. Your CD is probably earning about 5%. It may be cheaper to simply cash in the CD itself and use that money for the other investment.

Here's how to figure out whether you should cash in your CD or take a loan: First, find out how much interest you'll pay on a personal loan. Next, find out how much money you'll lose by cashing in your CD before its maturity date. Remember: You stand to lose the interest your money would have earned during the remainder of the CD's term, *plus* early withdrawal penalties, which range from 1 to 6 month's interest. Then, compare costs. (See Table 13.2.)

TABLE 13.2   BREAKING A CD VS. TAKING A LOAN

COST OF EARLY CD CASH-IN ($5,000 CD: 2 YEARS LEFT UNTIL MATURITY; EARNS 5% INTEREST ANNUALLY):

Interest Lost	$500
Prepayment Penalty	$262.50
Total Cost	$762.50

COST OF BORROWING A PERSONAL LOAN ($5,000 PERSONAL LOAN, FOR 2 YEARS, ANNUAL INTEREST RATE = 10%):

Interest Cost:	Year 1	$500
	Year 2	$500
Total Cost		$1,000

You should hold onto your CD and take a loan if:

- It costs less to take out the loan than to cash in the CD.

- Your CD is nearing its maturity date. You can always pay back the loan as soon as you cash in the CD.

- You have a hard time saving money. And this CD is your only savings account.

Borrowing Bonus If your CD is at a bank, you can usually borrow up to 100%. And there is no fee for borrowing against a CD.

Beware Bankspeak Loans against CDs aren't especially cheap, unless you fall for the misleading calculations that some people use to explain the cost of this loan. The cost of any loan is the interest rate—no matter how much your other investments at the same bank are earning.

In this lesson, you learned how to borrow against your life insurance policy and your certificates of deposit. In the next lesson, you will learn how to finance a small business.

14

FINANCING A SMALL BUSINESS

In this lesson, you'll learn how to get a commercial loan and an SBA loan.

START-UPS ARE RISKY

Being your own boss may sound inviting. At some point or another, you've probably dreamed about kissing the rat race goodbye, starting your own business, and—naturally—making a fortune in the process.

In fact, the sad truth is that 25% of all new start-up businesses close down within two years and 60% close within six years, according to the Small Business Administration. Those are not good odds, which is why many lenders will *not* do business with you until you have a proven track record as a successful entrepreneur.

Ask Relatives   Initially, many would-be entrepreneurs bypass the business loan altogether. To get your fledgling operation off the ground, you simply ask friends and family for a loan. Often, you'll look to your own resources, too, like tapping a Home Equity Line of Credit or taking out a second mortgage on your home.

Once the business is established and you can show a steady cash flow, you can look toward banks and other lenders if you need more money to buy additional machinery or expand into a new market. Your first stop for such funding will likely be a commercial bank.

LOANS FROM A COMMERCIAL BANK

Commercial banks grant all sizes of business loans, in addition to home mortgages. They charge a stated interest rate, too—plus points, which is generally the bank's commission for doing the deal.

It's no surprise, then, that many bankers are reluctant to grant loans for less than $100,000. (Of course, they'll tell you otherwise.) But the truth is they can make more money—doing the same amount of work—granting a $500,000 loan. So why not just ask for that extra capital up front? Larger amounts are difficult to secure if you don't have a track record as a business owner.

Still, banks do grant business loans to novice entrepreneurs. It depends largely upon your creditworthiness, cash flow, and collateral. Here's what a bank wants to see:

- A resume of the principals and managers of the proposed business. What is your professional background? For example, if you're opening up a kids' clothing shop, do you have prior retail experience?

- A business plan, including *realistic* financial projections. Banks will examine these numbers ever so carefully, so use a conservative figure for expected income, a liberal figure for expenses.

- Personal financial statements, listing your assets and liabilities. The bank wants to see what personal funds you have available to invest. They may even ask to review your tax returns for the past several years.

- How do you plan on supporting yourself? Banks will want to know if you plan on working another job until this business gets off the ground. Or, if you're a professional such as a dentist buying someone else's practice, will you work together for the first year to ease the change of ownership, so there'll be almost no noticeable dip in clients billed?

- Heavy collateral—including real estate, stocks, and bonds—to secure business loans. This is necessary unless you have substantial cash reserves of your own or an existing cash flow.

Rejected   An acceptable amount of collateral doesn't necessarily guarantee the approval of a bank loan. The key question on most bankers' minds is whether you can generate the cash flow needed to pay the loan back.

Your House at Risk   To secure a small business loan, you'll probably have to put up your house as collateral. If you default on your commercial loan, it's harder for the bank to actually seize your house. They must look to your business first to collect their debt. If you default on a home equity loan, however, the bank will seize your home automatically.

Small Business Administration (SBA) Loans

If you've been rejected by the bank, it's time to contact the Small Business Administration (SBA). The SBA is an agency of the Federal government that was established in 1953 to help small businesses get started, stay in business, and grow. Although people often talk about "SBA Loans," the agency doesn't lend its own money directly to consumers. Rather, you apply for an SBA loan through your commercial lender. The SBA then vouches for your creditworthiness by guaranteeing your loan at the bank—as much as 80% of the loan, up to a maximum of $750,000.

 Don't Pass Go   Some would-be business owners contact the SBA right away. Don't bother. In most cases, the SBA will only review your request if you have a loan rejection letter from a commercial lender attached to your application.

But why does the SBA like your financial prospects more than the local bank did? Simple. Rather than looking at collateral, like most banks do, the SBA looks at *cash flow* as the primary indicator of your creditworthiness. The SBA can't, in fact, turn down a loan solely because of lack of collateral.

The SBA does require some owner equity—usually 25% to 35% of the loan amount—which many people provide by pledging their house and/or some business assets.

Pink Slipped If you've been laid off recently, you may have additional funds at hand: your severance or early-retirement package and your 401(k) rollover. (You'll have to pay taxes and a penalty for early withdrawal).

In addition, SBA loans are more consumer-friendly because they're offered for longer terms: 5, 10, even 25 years. (The average SBA loan term is 11 years.)

To apply for an SBA loan, ask the bank (which just denied your loan request) if it'll provide the loan with an SBA guarantee. Some banks will even intercede with the SBA on your behalf. If not, contact your local SBA office and request a "loan packet." Included are booklets with information detailing how much money you can borrow, what the money can be used for, and a list of approved lenders you can contact.

To find the office nearest you, check the U.S. Government pages of your phone book or call the SBA Answer Desk at 800-8-ASK-SBA. The computer literate will find the SBA at *http://www.sbaonline.sba.gov.*

Preferred Lenders Commercial banks and other lenders that carry the SBA's "preferred" stamp of approval don't have to get agency approval before applying for an SBA-loan. Check with your district office for preferred lenders in your area.

MORE SBA PROGRAMS

Low Documentation Program. The major drawback of an SBA loan has always been the voluminous paperwork involved in the application itself. Recently, that hefty application has been cut to just one page under the "Low Documentation" program. The restrictions: You can't borrow more than $100,000 or have declared bankruptcy in the past.

Less Paperwork? Because it's just a one-page application, many banks are more willing than usual to work with the SBA. While this new "quickie" application may have been cut to just one page, you will still have to provide plenty of supporting documentation, such as your financial statements, tax returns, and business plan.

Women's Prequalification Loan Project. This is a pilot program currently being tested in some 15 cities. Women business owners apply to an intermediary, like a Small Business Development Center, recommended by the SBA. They help her package the loan application and then get it pre-approved by the SBA *before* she applies for a commercial loan. (An identical program, the *Minority Loan Prequalification Project*, is also offered for minorities.)

FA$TRAK. This is another pilot program being tested with 18 large banks. Supposedly, it saves time by cutting down on paperwork. Lenders use their own loan applications and procedures (instead of the SBA's) and apply directly to the SBA.

Service Corps of Retired Executives (SCORE). This is a free counseling program composed of 13,000 retired executives around the country, which can help you develop a business plan and answer other questions about setting up shop.

In this lesson, you learned how to get a commercial loan and an SBA loan. In the next lesson, you will learn how to arrange financing for a new or used car.

15

Financing a New or Used Car

In this lesson, you'll learn how to figure out what kind of car loan to use when you're buying a new or used automobile.

The Cost of a Car Today

The average price of a new car today is $20,000. Nearly 90% of all car buyers will use some form of borrowing when buying their next car.

While paying cash is the cheapest way to buy a car, few of you probably have the requisite cash just lying around. No doubt you've heard about some of the cost advantages of leasing. No down payment is required; you can afford a more expensive car; and you don't have the hassle of trading in your old clunker when you want a new car. This sounds great, but leasing isn't for everyone—especially if you drive a lot and tend to drive your car into the ground. (Read Lesson 16 for more about leasing.) You should probably consider the old-fashioned *auto loan*.

WHY IT'S CHEAPER TO PAY CASH

Lenders only make money when you *borrow* their money, so they may paint a distorted picture of loans as a smart investment. For example, let's assume you have $10,000 on hand. You could use that money to buy a car outright, or you could take out a four-year auto loan and invest that cash in a mutual fund. Let's further assume that you'd earn more in the mutual fund in four years than you'd pay out in interest charges. At first glance, taking out the auto loan seems like the better deal. However, how are you going to repay the car loan?

- Is the money coming out of earnings? Then you're using cash that would have been saved or invested elsewhere.

- Is the money coming out of savings? Then you're losing interest. That amount has to be subtracted from the interest earned on the mutual fund. Are you still earning more than you're spending?

The bottom line: It's cheaper to pay cash.

 Don't Wipe Yourself Out   Paying cash *is* the cheapest method of financing a car, but it's not a good strategy if it means wiping out your entire savings. You must keep an emergency cash reserve on hand.

DON'T STRETCH OUT YOUR PAYMENTS

The biggest cost of owning a car—if you're borrowing the money to make the purchase—is the interest incurred over the life of the loan. You probably never think about that. Instead, you worry about being able to afford the monthly car payment. So you stretch the loan term to five years instead of three.

That will certainly lower your monthly payments. Maybe it'll even let you buy a more expensive car than you could otherwise afford. But it'll cost you lots more in interest. Remember: The longer you borrow money, the more interest you'll pay. Plus, you'll be charged a higher rate of interest! (See Table 15.1.) The only way to keep interest costs down is to get a lower interest rate, shorten the term of the loan, or borrow less money.

TABLE 15.1   PAYMENTS FOR A $15,000 AUTO LOAN

LENGTH OF LOAN	INTEREST RATE	MONTHLY PAYMENTS	TOTAL INTEREST PAID
3-Year	6.95%	$462.81	$1,661.16
4-Year	7.90%	$365.49	$2,543.52
5-Year	8.25%	$305.94	$3,356.40

A car should be financed over the number of years you expect to drive it, or less if you can afford it. Here's why:

1. When you buy a car, you build up equity gradually. During the first three years, in fact, your car's net value is generally less than zero. If you take out a five-year loan but decide in three years that you want a newer model—or the car breaks down and you'd rather upgrade than spend money fixing this clunker—the resale value of the car isn't going to be enough to repay the loan in full. So you'll still have to make some payments.

2. Now you need another car. You'll probably have to borrow again. That means you'll have two auto loans outstanding, instead of one.

CREDIT UNIONS OFFER THE BEST RATES

It's generally cheaper to finance a new car through a credit union rather than a bank. Typically, the average interest rate at a credit union is a full point below the banks, and two points below auto dealers. (See Table 15.2.) If you don't currently belong to a credit union, now's the time to sign up. (See Lesson 3 for details.)

TABLE 15.2   AUTO LOAN INTEREST RATES*

TYPE OF LENDER	AVERAGE INTEREST RATE
Bank	9.26%*
Credit Union	8.08%*
Dealer	10.00%
Home Equity Line of Credit	8.61%*

Source: Bank Rate Monitor, North Palm Beach, FL

Bank auto loans, like almost every other type of loan, vary from lender to lender, so be sure to shop around. You can often knock a quarter to half a percentage point off the going rate if you already have a checking or savings account with that particular bank.

No Down Payment Traditionally, banks wanted a 10-20% down payment for an auto loan. Not anymore. Some banks now offer 100% financing.

Banks generally offer *simple interest* auto loans. Your payments stay the same every month. But, technically you're only paying interest each month on the amount of the loan that's outstanding. What you want to avoid, however, is a *front-end installment* loan. With this type of loan, you pay interest each month on the *total* amount that you borrowed. In the end, a front-end installment loan could cost you several thousand dollars more in interest than a simple interest loan.

Get Pre-Approved If you walk into a car dealership with a pre-approved bank loan in your hand, you're likely to get a better deal on the car itself because that tells the salesman that you're a "serious" buyer. He'll turn somersaults before letting you out the door without a sale.

Of course, you can always borrow money from the bank without actually taking out a car loan. Remember that old home equity line of credit? (See Lesson 8.) Unlike a traditional car loan, that line of credit is tax deductible. However, the only danger is that you could lose the car—and your house—if you default on your loan payments.

BORROWING FROM AN AUTO DEALER

Dealer financing almost always costs more than banks or credit unions. (See Table 15.2.) But if you buy a car during their periodic "discount days" promotions, you'll save a bundle in financing costs. Some of these deals are ridiculously low: 5% when the prevailing rate is 9%. As always, you have to watch the fine print. Frequently, the hot-selling and/or high-end models are not included in these money-saving deals.

Here are some other reasons to check out dealer financing:

- It's convenient. You pick a car and a loan in the very same place. Sometimes you can get a loan in 30 minutes or less.

- Dealers are more liberal about lending requirements. If your credit rating is questionable, this may be your only option.

- They offer sweet deals for certain buyers. Ford Motor Credit Company, General Motors Acceptance Corporation (GMAC), and the lending arms of other automakers offer special financing deals to first-time buyers, college-graduates, and other groups.

- You can "trade-in" your old jalopy as a down payment on the new car—without the hassle of selling the old car yourself through a classified ad.

Now for the drawbacks. You're still dealing with a car salesman. And if you haven't done your homework, you're sure to get a bad deal. Be sure to check out the auto loan rates that your local banks are currently offering *before* you step foot in a dealership. That way, when you do talk to the dealer, you can compare costs intelligently.

Second, don't, under any circumstances, talk about financing before you negotiate price. Most sales people will ask how you plan on paying for the car almost immediately. Tell him that you haven't decided yet. Why? If the salesperson knows you're going to use dealer financing, he or she may simply jack up the car's price to give you what looks like a lower interest rate.

BUYING A USED CAR

A brand new car depreciates (loses value) as soon as you drive it off the dealer's lot. That's why even a one-year-old car is worth substantially less than you paid for it fresh out of the factory. If you want to beat the high cost of depreciation, and save yourself some money, buy a used car instead of a new one.

Buyers have traditionally shied away from used cars because they didn't want to get stuck with someone else's transmission problems. But, nowadays dealers have lots of "good" used cars—vehicles that have just come off two- and three-year leases. In many cases, dealers are refurbishing these cars and offering extended warranties, much like those you get with a new car.

Higher Interest When you finance a used car, expect to pay a higher interest rate—about two to three percentage points more—than you'd be charged on a new car.

Still worried you'll get stuck with a lemon? Consult the National Automobile Dealers Association's *Official Used Car Guide*. It covers domestic and imported cars and trucks, and lists a used car's trade-in value, loan value (how much a typical bank will lend you to finance the car), and retail value.

In this lesson, you learned how to finance a new or used car. In the next lesson, you will learn how to lease a car.

16

SHOULD YOU LEASE OR BUY?

In this lesson, you'll learn how to lease a car.

It used to be that when you needed a new car, you paid for it. Or rather, you *borrowed* money to pay for it. Nowadays, however, you can no longer tax-deduct the interest on a car loan (or any other consumer loan, for that matter), so leasing has become a popular alternative to the conventional auto loan.

LEASING—ANOTHER WAY TO GET A CAR

When you use conventional financing to buy a car, you contract to pay, over a specified amount of time, the entire purchase price of the car—plus interest. (That's minus the value of a trade-in and/or a down payment, of course.) Once you've paid off the loan, you own the car.

In a typical car loan, a buyer often makes a 10 to 20% down payment on the total cost of the car, with the balance paid in 48 or 60 monthly installments at a fixed rate of interest. You'll also pay sales tax on the entire purchase price up front, which, depending on where you live, may run you several hundred dollars.

When you lease a car, however, you don't pay for the whole car, just the part you use. Therefore, your monthly payments should be lower—as much as 35% lower, in fact—than if you finance the purchase. Once the lease expires, you must give the car back. You do not own it.

Unlike a conventional auto loan, a lease requires no down payment. There are certain up-front fees and costs, however. Before you can drive the car out of the showroom, for instance, you generally must fork over your first month's payment as well as a refundable security deposit (another month's payment).

Capitalized Cost Reduction   In a lease agreement, a capitalized cost reduction is an initial cash outlay that works just like a down payment. Look for a lease without this feature. After all, no down payment is one of the major advantages of a lease.

You'll have to pay sales tax on a lease, too, but, unlike a loan, it's spread out over the life of your lease. This should put less strain on your cash flow, since you'll probably pay just a few extra dollars with each monthly payment rather than an initial lump-sum payment.

Registration and Licensing   These fees vary from state to state. It'll cost the same whether you buy or lease the car.

THE BASIC TERMS OF A LEASE AGREEMENT

Most lease agreements run for 36 or 48 months, although some are as long as 72 months and some as short as 12. Under no circumstances should you agree to a longer term than you want, because you'll be hit with a steep early-termination penalty.

 Beware the Five-Year Lease   Some dealers may try to rope you into a five-year lease because the monthly payments are so low. They may even tell you that there's no problem if you want to break the lease. Don't believe them. You'll have to pay the difference, which could amount to a few thousand dollars.

The cost of a lease is calculated by subtracting the residual value of the car from its original selling price, plus interest—in leasing vernacular this is called a *rental fee, money factor,* or *lease charge.*

 Residual Value   Residual value is an estimate of how much the car will be worth at the end of the lease period. Most lessors use a standard leasing guidebook, such as the *Automotive Lease Guide,* to determine a car's residual value.

Rental Fee   Rental fee is the interest rate charged on an auto lease. It generally runs close to the interest rate charged on auto loans.

Practically all leases have a maximum mileage limit—usually 15,000 miles per year—written into the lease agreement. Drivers who exceed the limit are charged approximately 10 to 15 cents for every extra mile logged over that limit.

Over the Limit   If you expect to drive more in a year than the amount stipulated in the lease contract, negotiate those extra miles up front. You'll get a cheaper rate.

NEGOTIATING THE PRICE

If you're planning to lease your car, shop around just as you would if you were actually purchasing the car. Check rates at banks, auto dealers, and independent leasing firms. Don't be afraid to negotiate. The purchase price, which is used by the leasing company to calculate lease payments, *is* negotiable. It's basically the sticker price, and you should *never* pay that.

Bargain for a Cheaper Lease   Haggle over the purchase price of the car first, then tell the dealer you're interested in leasing. You'll get a lower monthly payment.

If you think that you want to buy the car when your lease expires, make sure your contract includes a *purchase option*.

Not all leases do. At lease-end, the price of the car can be negotiated—much like the purchase price was. Some dealers automatically set this price at the residual value when you sign the lease. But other dealers let you leave the price open, to be determined by the car's "fair market value" when your lease contract expires. No matter how the purchase price is set, you can ultimately buy the car if it seems like a bargain—or just walk away if it doesn't.

Disposition Fee   Disposition fee covers the cost of getting the car ready for sale once you've returned it. Often it's deducted from your security deposit. If you buy the car, you shouldn't have to pay a disposition fee.

Moving?   If you're planning on moving out of state, check to see if there are any restrictions. Some lenders levy additional fees.

LEASING A "USED" CAR

In addition to leasing a new car, there's another option now available. You can lease a car that's already been leased.

Luxury sedans like a Mercedes or a Jaguar tend to depreciate slower than cheaper, more mainstream cars, so you might not find much of a bargain here—unless the car is at least four years old.

But some automakers do offer substantially lower monthly payments—even extended warranties and roadside assistance—for two- and three-year-old vehicles coming off a lease.

To find a good deal, scan the newspaper ads or contact the auto dealer directly. Many of them now run special programs for leasing used cars.

LEASING VS. BUYING

Over the long haul, buying—whether you're paying cash or taking out an auto loan—is *still* the cheapest option because ultimately you own the car. (See Table 16.1.) And once you've paid off that auto loan—especially if you take a three- or four-year loan—it's likely that you could then drive the car some years thereafter for free (depending, of course, on how much you drive and how well you take care of your car). With leasing, you must give back the car. You could always buy the car at lease-end, but it's not always worth it.

The difference in costs between financing and leasing varies widely, according to the term length and the type of vehicle that you buy. Unfortunately, there is no one right answer. Leasing and financing are simply two different ways to pay for the car that you drive. And, as you've done with other funds that you've borrowed, you'll have to comparison-shop to find the best deal.

TABLE 16.1 LEASING VS. FINANCING

	LEASING	FINANCING
Term	36 Months	36 Months
Manufacturer's Sugg. Retail Price	$12,000.00	$12,000.00
Down Payment	$0.00	$2,400.00
Monthly Payment	$225.00	$250.00

	LEASING	FINANCING
Amount Paid	$8,100.00	$9,000.00
Amount Owed (at Term End)*	$6,500.00	$0.00
Total Cost of the Car	$14,600.00	$11,400.00

* If the customer wished to purchase the leased car.

Leasing is a good alternative if:

- You don't want to tie up your ready cash in a depreciating asset. Instead, take the money not used for a down payment and the money saved from lower monthly payments and invest it elsewhere.

- You'd like to change cars every 2 or 3 years, but you can't afford to buy a new car that often.

- You drive less than 15,000 miles every year.

- You have just enough money for a down payment, but you also have large balances on your credit cards. You're better off leasing a car and using the down payment money to pay off the credit card bill.

- You want to drive a more expensive car than you can afford to buy.

- You want to leave your credit free for other loans. Unlike conventional auto loans, leasing contracts generally aren't listed on a loan application.

- You're short on funds, but your cash flow is good.

In this lesson, you learned how to lease a car. In the next lesson, you will learn how much interest you can tax-deduct on consumer loans, commercial loans, and home mortgages.

17

Your Tax Deduction on Home Mortgages and Other Loans

In this lesson, you'll learn how much interest you can tax-deduct on consumer loans, commercial loans, and home mortgages.

Taxes can make your head spin. The mortgage interest paid on a $1.5 million home isn't fully deductible—but the interest paid on a $50,000 cabin cruiser is. Unless you took out the mortgage on that mansion before 1987, the interest paid on the house *is* fully deductible. And the cabin cruiser? If you own that mansion, plus a beachfront condo on Martha's Vineyard *and* that cabin cruiser, the interest paid on the boat isn't deductible.

In this lesson and the next one, the basic deductions for certain kinds of loans are outlined. For more details, call the IRS or ask your tax advisor.

Consumer Loans

There is no tax deduction *at all* for interest paid on consumer loans. This includes:

- personal loans
- auto loans
- credit card debt
- student loans

A Loophole   You can deduct the interest paid on your credit card debt *if* you consolidate that credit card debt through a home equity line of credit (HELOC). The interest paid on a HELOC is fully deductible on loans up to $100,000.

COMMERCIAL LOANS

What if you borrow money to start up a business? You can deduct *all* the interest on a commercial loan. If you're the sole proprietor of the business, you would file a Schedule C: The interest deduction for your commercial loan would reduce your business's gross income—in other words, the TAXABLE amount.

Any Loan Will Do   Interest is deductible as a business expense on any kind of loan—it doesn't have to be a commercial loan—as long as you use the money to start or expand a business.

HOME MORTGAGES

The rules on deducting interest for home mortgages are more complicated. What you can deduct (and how much) depends on whether the house is a primary residence or a vacation home, how much you've borrowed (and for what purpose), and whether it's a first mortgage, a home equity loan, or a refinancing.

POINTS

According to the Internal Revenue Service, you can fully deduct all the mortgage points paid on your home mortgage in the year that you buy a house if:

- You use the loan to buy or build your primary residence. (Your primary residence is the one you live in most of the time.)

- The points paid were not more than the points generally charged in that area.

- The points were computed as a percentage of the debt, rather than a flat fee.

- You didn't pay points instead of other fees listed separately on the settlement statement, such as appraisal fees, inspection fees, title fees, attorney fees, and property taxes.

- You paid the points out of your own funds. That's true if your down payment, escrow deposit, or any other monies paid at or before closing cost are at least as much as the points charged.

- You paid points to a mortgage broker. They're fully deductible.

 Points Paid by Seller Points sometimes include *loan placement fees* that the seller pays the lender to arrange financing for the buyer. The seller *cannot* deduct these fees as interest, but the buyer can, just as if he or she had actually paid them.

Mortgage Ending Early   If you spread your deduction for points over the life of the mortgage, you can deduct the remaining "points" balance (if there is one) in the year that the mortgage ends.

MORTGAGE INTEREST

Mortgage interest is any interest paid on a loan secured by your home (that includes primary residences and second homes, too). The loan may be a mortgage to buy your home, a home equity loan, or a home equity line of credit.

You can fully deduct all of the mortgage interest paid on your home if:

- You took out your mortgage on or before October 13, 1987 (called *grandfathered* debt).

- Your total mortgage debt equals $1 million or less on your regular house and vacation home(s) combined. If you're married but filing separately, the limit is $500,000 or less. (This applies if you got your mortgage after 1987.)

No Tax-Free Deductions   You can't deduct your home mortgage interest if you used the borrowed money to buy securities or certificates that produce tax-free income.

Some mortgages have *graduated payments*. (See Lesson 5 for a full explanation.) During the early years, payments are less than the amount of interest owed on the loan. The interest that is not paid becomes part of the principal, and future interest is figured on the increased unpaid mortgage loan balance.

You can still deduct the interest, but only the amount that you paid rather than the amount you actually owe. For instance: The interest owed on your graduated-payment loan is $2,551 this year, but your payments totaled just $2,517. You can deduct $2,517 on your taxes.

Extra Interest Payments   You can deduct late mortgage payment charges and any mortgage prepayment penalties as home mortgage interest.

When you buy a home in some states (Maryland, for example), you must pay a *ground rent*. You can deduct these payments as mortgage interest, too, if your lease is for more than 15 years *and* you can buy out the lease in the future.

Ground Rent   Ground rent is a fixed amount that is paid annually or periodically for the use of property. You're leasing (rather than buying) the land on which your home is built.

Where to Deduct Your Interest   Deduct home mortgage interest and points on Schedule A, line 10.

A Second Home

What classifies as a home these days? According to the IRS, any place where you can sleep, cook, and use the toilet is a home. That includes condomimiums, co-ops, trailers, and even boats.

You can deduct mortgage interest paid on a first home and *one* second home, if you don't rent your vacation home out to other people. It doesn't matter how frequently you live at the house during the year. (In fact, you never have to use it to qualify for the deduction.)

Once you start renting that second house, however, the equation changes. To qualify for a mortgage interest deduction, you have to occupy your second home for at least 14 days, or 10% more than your paying tenants do, whichever is longer.

If you don't, the house is considered a rental property (rather than a second home) and you have to report that rent as income. Most likely, you'll still be able to write off the interest deductions—plus you can then deduct rental expenses. (See Lesson 18 for more details on real estate investment deductions.)

What about points? Points paid on loans for a second home must be deducted over the life of the loan instead of in a lump sum the year that you buy it.

More Deductions   If you rent your vacation home for part of the year, you may be able to deduct your financing fees as a cost of doing business. That includes your closing costs, attorney's fees, and bank charges.

REFINANCING

You can't write off all the points that you pay for a refinancing in the first year. They have to be deducted over the life of the loan—unless you use some of the borrowed money for home improvements.

For example: If you use 25% of the money borrowed through the refinancing to remodel the kitchen or to fix that leaky roof, you can then deduct 25% of the points in the very same year that you paid them.

HOME EQUITY LOANS

You can write off 100% of the interest paid on a home equity loan (also known as a "second mortgage") or a home equity line of credit (HELOC) for loans up to $100,000. (If you're married but filing separately, it's $50,000.) The loan amount, however, cannot exceed your home's fair market value.

 Fair Market Value   The fair market value of your home is the price at which you could reasonably expect to sell your home should you put it up for sale tomorrow.

Interest on amounts over this $100,000/fair-market-value limit are not deductible *unless* you use the loan for an investment or to finance a business. Then it's fully deductible again, as a business or investment expense.

In this lesson, you learned how much interest you can tax-deduct on consumer loans, commercial loans, and home mortgages. In the next lesson, you will learn how much interest you can tax-deduct on investment loans.

LESSON

18

YOUR TAX DEDUCTION ON LOANS FOR INVESTMENT

In this lesson, you will learn how much interest you can tax-deduct on loans made for investment.

INTEREST DEDUCTIONS ON MONEY USED FOR INVESTING

You can take out just about any kind of loan—a personal loan, a margin loan, even a home equity line of credit—and use that money to buy stocks, bonds, or mutual funds. As long as you make an *investment* with that borrowed money, you can often tax-deduct the interest paid on the loan.

You can deduct the interest on your investment loan if you have a *net income* from those investments. You may deduct as much in interest costs as your investments produce in net income.

Let's say your investments paid $3,000 (net) in interest and dividends last year. That means you can write off $3,000 of the interest paid on your investment loans. If you spent more in interest than you earned in dividends this year, however, you can carry forward the surplus and deduct it next year.

Net Investment Income   Net investment income is a dividend and/or interest earned on your investments *minus* expenses (except interest). In other words, your *net taxable income*.

CALCULATING INVESTMENT INCOME AND EXPENSES

To calculate your investment income, you can deduct certain expenses that you incur in connection with your investments, such as:

- Fees that you pay your broker or banker for investment advice and to collect income, such as the interest earned on your taxable bonds or the dividends paid on your stocks. You *cannot*, however, deduct the fees paid to a broker (or any other agent) to buy or sell the investment itself.

- The rent that you pay on a safe-deposit box—if you use the box to store taxable income-producing stocks and bonds or investment-related documents. The catch: You can't deduct all of the rent if you also use the box to store personal items or tax-exempt securities.

- The service charge for reinvesting your dividends. Some companies take out a service charge from your cash dividends before those dividends are reinvested in more stock.

- Office expenses, such as rent and clerical help, that pertain to your investments.

You *cannot*, however, deduct the following as investment expenses:

- Transportation and other expenses incurred to attend a stockholders' meeting.

- Expenses incurred to attend a convention, seminar, or similar meeting for investment purposes.

- The interest paid on a loan which you used to buy single-premium life insurance or tax-exempt bonds.

 Form 1040   To itemize your investment expenses, use Schedule A on Form 1040. Your investment "interest" expense goes on Schedule A, too, on line 13.

Now comes the tricky part. What if you borrow $10,000 on margin, and use the money for different purposes: $2,000 to buy some stocks, for example, and $8,000 to buy a used car? Can you still deduct the interest?

The money that you borrowed has been used to make a consumer purchase as well as an investment, so you have to divvy up the debt on your taxes, too. That means, the interest paid on the money you used to buy the stocks *is* deductible—up to the investment's net income. But, the interest paid on the money you used to buy the car is *not* deductible because the margin loan is working like a consumer loan. And, interest on consumer loans is never deductible (see Lesson 17), *unless*

- You borrow that $10,000 through a home equity line of credit (HELOC). Then, no matter if you invest the borrowed money in stocks or blow it all on a new convertible, all the interest is deductible—up to $100,000.

- You invest the money in tax-exempt bonds, instead of stocks. Then you can't deduct the investment interest at all.

 Set Up Separate Accounts   When you borrow money for more than one purpose, put the loan proceeds into separate accounts so that it'll be clear how much interest can be tax-deducted on that loan. For instance, set up one account for personal borrowing (which is not deductible), another for investment borrowing, and another for business borrowing (both of which are deductible).

DEDUCTIONS FOR MARGIN LOANS AND RETIREMENT PLANS

You can deduct the interest paid on margin loans in the year that you pay it. According to the IRS, you have paid interest on a margin loan if:

1. You've actually paid the broker directly. (Your cancelled check is your receipt.)

2. Your broker has used the interest available in your account. (Payment of interest should be noted on receipts of securities bought and sold or dividends earned.)

If you borrow money from your company retirement plan you can probably tax-deduct the interest if you invest the money or use it to fund a business. But you must borrow your employer's contributions, not your pre-tax dollars (or any of the money earned on those pre-tax dollars). If you contribute after-tax money to the plan—and that's the money you borrow—you'll qualify for an interest deduction, too.

 IRA Contributions You can't claim an interest deduction on money borrowed to fund an Individual Retirement Account.

Deductions for Vacation Home Rentals

You and your family own a second home and vacation there periodically, but to help defray some of the cost of maintaining a second home, you rent it to others. This vacation home is rented, in fact, for more days than you or your family actually use it. (See Lesson 17 for the precise rules.) It now qualifies as a *rental property*.

So what's your tax deduction? Like most other home mortgage interest, the interest paid on a rental property is deductible. In addition, you can tax-deduct some of the expenses incurred in renting that home, such as:

- The cost of repairs. Fixing gutters or leaks, plastering, and replacing broken windows, or any other maintenance work that keeps your property in good working order qualifies as a "repair." Home improvements do not. You *cannot* deduct the cost of adding another bathroom, putting up a fence, or paving a driveway.

* Advertising, janitorial and maid services, utilities, fire and liability insurance, commissions paid for the collection of rent, some travel expenses, and water, sewer, and trash collection fees.

You can't deduct 100% of those expenses, however, if you use the home occasionally, too. You must divide the expenses paid on a rental property—as we did with investment interest paid earlier—between rental use and personal use.

 File Here   The IRS says it's okay if your deductible rental expenses exceed your gross rental income. Report both your rental income and rental expenses on Form 1040, Schedule E, *Supplemental Income and Loss.*

In this lesson you learned how much interest you can tax deduct on loans made for investment. In the next lesson, you will learn how to check your credit report, fix errors, and boost your chances for credit approval.

19

IF YOU'RE TURNED DOWN FOR A LOAN

In this lesson, you'll learn how to check your credit report, fix errors, and boost your chances for credit approval.

THE APPLICATION PROCESS

When you apply for a loan, lenders want to know if you're a good risk. Whom do you currently owe money to—and how much? Do you make your payments on time? When did you make your last payment? Often, lenders get those answers by reviewing a potential borrower's *consumer credit report*. Compiled by three nationwide credit bureaus, these reports can make—or break—your chances to borrow money.

The average credit report contains information about:

1. **Your Identity.** Your name and address (previous and current), plus your social security number and employment history.

2. **Your Credit History.** Details about your loans, lines of credit, and credit card accounts, such as account balances, credit limits, loan amounts, and how you've paid your accounts over the past two years.

3. **Your Public Record.** Any court records related to bankruptcies or tax liens. In some states, credit reports list delinquent child support payments, too.

 Not Included   Credit reports don't report every financial peccadillo. Generally overlooked are hospital and doctor bills, as well as charge accounts with utility and oil companies, and accounts at small retail shops.

CHECKING YOUR CREDIT REPORT

If you're planning to apply for a loan, it's smart to review your credit report *in advance* to be sure it's complete and accurate. Since most large creditors report their customer's bill-paying patterns to all three credit bureaus, you'll probably need to contact just one of them—either in writing or on the telephone.

Here's where to contact them:

TRW Information Systems and Services
National Consumer Assistance Center
P.O. Box 949
Allen, TX 75002
(800) 682-7654

Equifax
Credit Information Services
P.O. Box 105873
Atlanta, GA 30348
(800) 685-1111

Trans Union Corporation
P.O. Box 390
Springfield, PA 19064
(216) 779-7200

Be sure to include the following information with your request: your full name, social security number, current address, date of birth, and spouse's name.

 Get Your Free Copy   Residents of Maryland and Vermont can get one free copy of their report each year, as can all consumers who apply to TRW. The other bureaus charge $5 to $20 per copy.

If, after reviewing your credit file, you find an error, contact the bureau immediately and ask them to investigate the matter. Send any evidence, such as a paid invoice or a cancelled check, which will prove that their information is wrong.

By law, a credit bureau has to get back to you within a reasonable amount of time—generally 30 days—to tell you the results of their investigation. If they can't verify the information—or if an error was indeed made—they'll remove it from your file.

 Be Thorough   Once you have corrected the mistake at one credit bureau, ask for the change to be reported to the other two bureaus. Otherwise, the error may continue to show up on future reports.

What if you say you're right, and they say you're wrong? You can insert a written explanation (100 words or less) of your side of the story. Surprisingly, lenders do read these explanations.

Tell It to the Creditor Did you fall behind on payments because you lost your job or were going through a nasty divorce? You can add an explanatory statement to your file about those matters, too. It won't make those black marks go away, but it will show that you're generally responsible—despite some past problems.

What Went Wrong?

The bureau's job is to gather your financial history and report it to the people who are going to lend you the money. However, the bureau does *not* rate your creditworthiness. That's up to the individual lender. And even then there are no hard and fast rules.

Some lenders place more emphasis on income and job security—items that aren't even available in a credit report. (They're generally given on a loan application.) Others want to see how much unused credit you have and if you pay your bills on time. Quite simply, some lenders will give you the moon and others won't give you the time of day.

What lenders absolutely don't want to see on a credit report:

- You went bankrupt.

- You have a tax lien against your property.

- You were sued for past debts.

- You've applied for a lot of credit lately. (They think you're going to go deep in debt—perhaps so deep you won't be able to pay your bills.)

- You've been hounded by collection agencies to pay some bills.

If you're denied a loan because of information listed in your credit report, contact the bureau that processed your file *immediately*, to find out what went wrong. (You'll find their name and location in the letter from your lender, denying your application.) If you contact the bureau within 30 days of your credit denial, you'll get a free copy of your report.

Most of the information in a credit report comes directly from your current creditors. Sometimes they make mistakes. A clerk, for example, might make a typographical error or misread the account number written on a check. Perhaps your last three payments have been applied to someone else's account. The record would show that you're delinquent.

The credit bureau itself may be responsible for the error, too. Is the Jean Marie Bennett living in Tampa in 1988 the same Jean Marie Bennett living in Fort Lauderdale in 1995? Is the Dan Thompson on Horton Street the same as the Dan Thompson on Horton Avenue?

Occasionally, the consumer confuses matters by applying for a loan under different names, i.e., Robert and Bob, or Margaret and Peg. Others give the wrong social security number when applying for credit, or omit "senior" or "junior," when a father and son share the same name.

Best Bet   The surest way to prevent mixups is to use your correct social security number on all applications. Since that exact number is not assigned to anyone else, it'll keep you from being mistaken for someone with the same name.

BEWARE OF "CREDIT CLINICS"

"Turned down because of bad credit! We can help!" These supposed miracle-cures are advertised on late night television by credit clinics (also known as credit repair organizations), who claim that they can remove negative information from your credit report. Don't believe them.

These companies often operate on the fringe of legitimacy. Basically, they flood the credit bureaus with requests for information about your file. If the credit bureau can't respond to all these requests within a mandated time frame, the bad marks are supposedly erased.

What the clinics don't tell you, however, is that the credit bureau can later verify that information (when it has more time) and put those bad marks right back on your credit report. So you'll wind up with the same bad credit rap—*and* you'll be out the $50 to $2,000 fee that a clinic generally charges.

Do It Yourself   As a consumer, you can dispute inaccurate information on a credit report yourself—at no charge. But, unfortunately, there are no quick fixes. Only time can heal bad credit.

Follow Up   State law prevents past errors from haunting you forever. Tax liens and lawsuits are erased seven years after the information was entered; bankruptcy after 10 years. However, credit bureaus aren't always that prompt in erasing this stuff, even after the allotted time. Make sure that they do by asking for a follow-up report.

IMPROVE YOUR CHANCES OF GETTING APPROVED

Get your credit in order six months *before* applying for a loan. Try these tactics:

- Pay down some of your debt. The ideal: Your debts (including mortgages) should be less than 35% of your gross monthly income.

- Don't overextend yourself. Every credit card should not be "maxed" to the limit. Why? The more credit you're actively using, the higher the risk you are to lenders.

- Cancel some credit cards. This is especially good advice if you have a wallet full of every store, gas, and bank card imaginable. Get rid of cards that you rarely use or those that duplicate services, i.e., do you really need *two* Visa cards?

- Pay your bills on time—starting now. Most lenders don't care if your payments are up to 30 days late. But if your payments are further behind than that, catch up now—before you apply.

- Get a copy of your credit report and correct any errors. It couldn't happen to *your* report? One in four credit reports contain errors.

In this lesson, you learned how to check your credit report, fix errors, and boost your chances of approval. In the next lesson, you will learn what to do if you can't pay back your loan.

20

WHEN YOU CAN'T PAY YOUR LOAN

In this lesson, you'll learn how to manage your debt.

BORROWING SMARTLY

You've borrowed a great deal of money. Hopefully, you've applied the principles learned in this book and made smart, sound buys with that borrowed cash. Then again, maybe you haven't. But everyone makes mistakes.

If you're living beyond your means—that means spending more than you're earning, using up all your savings, and relying on credit to get by—the worst thing to do is run and hide. The only solution is to face your creditors and dig yourself out of debt.

OVER YOUR HEAD IN DEBT

The first place to start? Decrease your spending. That means stop purchasing with credit NOW. If you keep adding more and more debt, you'll just be digging an even deeper hole to get yourself out of. Try to adopt a pay-as-you-go spending style.

Next, consider a debt-consolidation loan. It will do the following:

- Immediately pay off all your creditors.

- Simplify bill paying.

- Get rid of nagging collection agencies.

- Lower your total monthly payment.

Debt-Consolidation Loan   A debt-consolidation loan is a loan that "consolidates" all of your debt—for most people that's credit card balances, but it can also include a personal loan from a credit union or a bank, even doctor's bills—and pays it off. You, the borrower, then make just one monthly payment to the lender. A home mortgage is not included.

Obviously, you must shop around for a good interest rate on the loan. Your new monthly payment should cost less than all of your individual monthly payments combined. Otherwise, why bother? All you've done is cut down on the number of checks you write each month, but you haven't saved any money.

Home Equity   Don't forget that home equity line of credit. It can be used for a debt-consolidation loan (see Lesson 6). Plus, it's tax-deductible.

Don't Consolidate   If you can't control your spending, you're likely to just run up those credit card balances again. Then you'll have two credit card debts—the consolidation loan and your current credit card balances—to pay back.

You've stretched and stretched that budget, but you just can't meet your monthly payments? Contact your creditors directly and tell them what's going on, i.e., "I lost my job in September and I'm having some difficulty meeting my monthly payments." Explain how much cash you currently have available to pay your bills and how many *other* creditors you have (and how much money you owe them). Lenders hate bankruptcy, so they're usually happy to work with you to arrange some sort of repayment plan. Suggest, for instance, that you'll repay each creditor $50 per month until your debt is paid off.

CREDIT COUNSELING

Your best bet for professional help is to contact the National Foundation for Consumer Credit, a reputable, nonprofit organization with some 1,100 *free or low-cost* Consumer Credit Counseling Service offices throughout the U.S. and Canada. Contact the organization at 800-388-2227 for the office in your area.

What will they do? They'll create a workable budget and repayment plan for you. Then, if necessary, they'll contact your creditors to arrange a new payment schedule. Generally, you'll make one monthly payment to the counseling service, out of which the service pays the creditors.

Credit Education   Bankcard Holders of America is a nonprofit, consumer organization that offers some great, low-cost pamphlets on managing debt and credit problems, such as "How to Get a Low-Interest-Rate Credit Card" and "Credit Cards: What You Don't Know Can Cost You." For information on membership and costs, contact them at: 524 Branch Drive, Salem, VA 24153; 703-389-5445.

FILING FOR BANKRUPTCY

You've tried *everything*. Your creditors won't accept an alternate payment plan. You can't get a debt-consolidation loan. Even a credit counselor couldn't get your bills aligned. Meanwhile, your phone just keeps ringing and ringing. It's one nasty bill collector after another, insisting upon full payment *now*—or else. You may have to file for bankruptcy.

There are two ways of filing for bankruptcy, both of which will stop your creditors from hounding you and protect you against wage garnishment. Both bankruptcy filings are complicated, however, so it's wise to consult an attorney who specializes in bankruptcy.

Here's a summary of each type of bankrutpcy filing:

1. *Chapter 13*
   The "wage-earner's bankruptcy" plan is for people with steady incomes, who could basically pay off their debts if they were granted an extension. The bankruptcy court works out a formal, debt-payment plan for you, over a three-to-five-year period. Usually, you make periodic payments to a court-appointed trustee, who then pays your creditors.

Chapter 11   Chapter 11 is another type of bankruptcy filing. Similar to Chapter 13, it's the bankruptcy filing for businesses.

Income that can't be touched generally includes: annuities, disability benefits, pension plans, alimony, child support, unemployment compensation, social security, veteran's benefits, and life insurance.

The Better Alternative   Creditors look more kindly upon a Chapter 13 bankruptcy than the Chapter 7 variety, so it'll be easier to reestablish credit in the future.

2. *Chapter 7*

   The "straight bankruptcy" plan gets rid of all debts (except most taxes, alimony payments, child support, and student loans), so you can essentially start your financial life all over again. Unfortunately, this usually entails selling most of your assets (like your house, diamond jewelry, etc.) and distributing the proceeds among your creditors.

Chapter 7   Chapter 7 is the most severe bankruptcy filing for individuals. It means liquidating almost all of your assets.

State Exemptions   Assets that can't be touched through a Chapter 7 bankruptcy filing vary by state. Most states let you keep personal belongings, such as a wedding ring and your used furniture. Others may even let you keep your car.

Additional debts that are not discharged under a Chapter 7:

1. Consumer loans over $500—if the money is owed to a single creditor, incurred for luxury items or services within 40 days of your bankruptcy filing.

2. Cash advances for more than $1,000—if the money is taken from an "open" credit plan within 20 days of your bankruptcy filing.

 Filing Again? You can file a new Chapter 13 if you've completed all the payments on your old Chapter 13. But you can file a Chapter 7 only once every six years.

The disadvantages to bankruptcy filing:

- It stays on your credit report for 10 years. After that time it drops off your record, but potential creditors can research farther back into your file if you're applying for a big loan.

- Generally, your credit cards are revoked.

- When you're ready to borrow money again, you'll generally have to pay the highest interest rate.

- The only credit card you'll qualify for after declaring bankruptcy is a *secured* credit card, which charges steep interest rates and requires a deposit with the underwriting bank.

In this lesson, you learned how to manage your debt. By now, you should be able to make smarter decisions about when to borrow, and how to choose a lender, the type of loan, and the terms of a loan.

INDEX